second touch of Jesus

By Jill Lowry

ISBN -13: 978-1-7371825-0-4

Second Touch of Jesus

www.jilllowryministries.com

Cover Design by Kerry Prater.

The events and conversations in this book have been set down to the best of the author's ability, although some names and details have been changed to protect the privacy of individuals. Some parts have been fictionalized in varying degrees, for various purposes.

Dedication

This book is dedicated to each person who desires to grow their faith through a deeper relationship with Jesus. My hope is that this book encourages you to share your story of faith, just as I am with you.

I want to thank my husband and children who love me and support me in all that I do. I am so blessed to have you all by my side praying with me.

I want to thank my father who read stories to me about the love of Jesus. This book begins with these stories of love he read to me so I could find Jesus.

And I want to thank my sister, Jennifer, for being by my side and loving me.

I want to thank my friend, editor, and author, Katharine Hamilton, who has helped me in so many ways. I covet your prayers, guidance, and encouragement.

Thank you to my beta readers and friends, Leslie and Tonya, for their honest feedback and taking the time to read this for me. I appreciate your support and encouragement.

And many thanks to every believer God placed in my life at various times in my journey. Each time you witnessed, I was brought closer to the love and grace of Jesus.

I have decided to follow Jesus!

HIS *reach*,
RESCUE,
and
restoration

Introduction

When I read a book, I like to know more about the author and his or her personal stories. When I read books about faith, I especially enjoy reading about personal testimonies of faith from the author. With that in mind, I decided to share my personal story so that you can know how the touches of Jesus have changed my life. I have lived *without* Jesus and I have lived *with* Him. I know what it feels like to be alone and what it feels like to be secure in Christ. I have felt the emptiness that comes with not having the saving grace of Jesus. However, I have experienced life with complete joy and the spiritual blessings given from the Holy Spirit when I let Jesus work through me. I am sharing my story for God's glory so that you can be encouraged in your own faith journey. This life-changing experience is possible for all who choose to receive Jesus Christ as their Savior and embrace His touches on their hearts!

I grew up with a little knowledge of Jesus but did not know him on a spiritual level. I did not know his touch on my heart or what a personal relationship with him meant. But Jesus was reaching for me from the start. However, I was the one controlling just how much I let Him live in my heart. Though He created me to love Him, made me in His image, and knitted me together in my mother's womb, He gave me the *choice* to love Him. I did not ask Jesus into my heart or ask for forgiveness of my sins for the first eighteen years of my life. I was living in my own power and control. I had not proclaimed Jesus as my Lord and Savior by inviting Him to live inside me and help me navigate decisions. I had not accepted His abiding love for me. **I did not have eternal life in Christ.**

My childhood was filled with an abundance of love and happiness from those close to me and I thought all was good. I tried to follow the rules and do good to others, but I repeatedly failed. I believed all good people would go to heaven, and I thought I was one of those good people. After all, I tried to do the right thing most of the time. I thought it was fine to let others influence me and, therefore, I became a follower to find security and confidence. I had friends and family who loved and supported me, but I still felt something missing. I could not figure out why I felt insecure even though I knew I was loved. Underneath the insecurity, there was an empty space void of joy. I searched to fill it with everyone else but Jesus. I put my hope in people and not a Savior. I had no idea that the missing piece was Jesus Himself.

He was right there beside me the entire time, too, waiting for me to find all that I needed in Him. He longed for me to *know* Him. He didn't force Himself into my life but tenderly reached for me through the first eighteen years. I had numerous questions that, later, would be answered in the pages of my Bible. This book is filled with these scriptures so you can read them as well. You will see how Jesus spoke truth to me from the very beginning. He is still sharing truth with me today as I read His love letters, His Word. He is speaking truth to you as well.

"For you formed my inward parts; you knitted me together in my mother's womb. I praise you, for I am fearfully and wonderfully made..."
Psalm 139:13-14

*"You will seek me and find me, when you seek me
with all your heart."
Jeremiah 29:13*

My first introduction to Jesus was as an early adolescent when I went to east Texas for the summer to visit my grandparents and aunts and attended their church with them. I listened to Bible stories in Sunday School and wondered how they applied to my life. I remember something inside of me felt different when I attended that little Methodist church in Overton, Texas, where my father grew up. And I enjoyed hearing about Jesus and how to be born again through Him. I wanted to know more, but I didn't fully understand His Word and His promises within it. When I'd head home from those trips to east Texas, I questioned how my sins could ever be forgiven because I couldn't even forgive myself. My sin and shame had such control over me, but I desperately wanted to be set free.

*"Jesus answered him, 'Truly, truly, I say to you, unless
one is born again he cannot see the kingdom of God.' "
John 3:3*

The only other knowledge I had about Jesus came from my father and the big, blue, children's Bible storybook he read to me and my little sister right before we went to sleep when I was young. These stories comforted me. I loved hearing my father's soft, soothing voice telling these stories. Stories that touched my heart and wrapped me, in not only his love, but also the love of Jesus.

I had trouble sleeping soundly as a child. I feared the dark, and that fear kept me awake most nights. But when I would see my father reach for that big, blue book, and hear him start to read, I felt a peace deep in my soul, that I did not quite understand, but knew I needed. As I snuggled up with all my stuffed animals and wrapped up in my Holly Hobbie comforter, I listened closely. The darkness vanished out of my mind, and I focused on the love I felt with each new story. My fears and troubles of the day disappeared, and I'd drift off to sleep in peace.

"Peace, I leave with you; my peace I give to you. Not as the world gives do I give to you. Let not your hearts be troubled, neither let them be afraid."
John 14:27

These Bible stories read by my father not only gave me peace but shaped the first details of Jesus in my mind and in my heart. I envisioned Jesus as a good friend. I believed he could heal certain people and perform miracles for the ones who knew him well. I grew to know the love of Jesus from the outside looking in as my father opened this treasured book each night. However, I felt out of touch because I did not know Jesus like the people did within the pages. I wasn't even sure I was worthy of his love. I did not consider Him my friend, but I wanted to. Jesus was present in the stories, but not present in my heart.

We will begin here in *this* book to see how the rest of my story unfolds. This is where I began my journey with Jesus and let Him touch my heart. This is when he reached for me the first time.

"O LORD, you have searched me and known me! You know when I sit down and rise up; you discern my thoughts from afar."
Psalm 139:1-2

HIS
reach

The Reach of Jesus Through my Father's Love

"It's time for bed," my dad called, as I finished drinking the colorful cupful of milk with ice. He always mixed my favorite bedtime drink with the cubed ice from the trays in the freezer, just the way I liked it. A little ice, a little milk, and a full tummy to ensure a good night's sleep awaited me each night. I loved drinking this right before I brushed and flossed my teeth and went to bed.

"I am ready for my story!" I yelled, as I finished up in the bathroom and darted towards my bed in a full leap that rivaled even the best gymnasts— full of bounce and eager excitement. "I'm not tired yet, so there's plenty of time for you to read to me, Daddy."

My dad purchased a big, blue children's Bible storybook to read to my sister and me so that we could grow together in our knowledge of the Bible.

"I am ready for bed too," Jennifer said, as she agreed to come to my room, as it was *my turn* for Daddy to read to us from the comfort of my own bed. My dad always made sure to treat us fairly, even when it came to reading nightly stories. We looked forward to hearing what he would pick out for the night. My sister, Jennifer, liking orange juice before bed, had just finished her drink, brushing and flossing her teeth, and making the same artful jump onto my bed as I had. "Hurry up, Daddy!" she squealed. "We are both ready and excited to hear our favorite story again tonight."

"Which story is that?" my dad asked.

"The one about Jesus healing people," I replied.

Jill Lowry

"There are lots of stories about Jesus healing people in the Bible, so which one are you wanting to hear tonight?"

"Can we hear about the people with the skin spots?" Jennifer asked.

"You mean the lepers." I corrected. As the older sister, acting like I knew more than she did came easily. I always remembered the word leper because my heart felt sorry for these isolated people who felt so helpless. I couldn't imagine what it must have been like to be a leper. My heart saddened for the lepers because at times I, too, felt isolated and different. See, I didn't live with both of my parents like most of my friends. My parents were divorced, and I felt insecure because of it. Knowing the reality of insecurity, I listened with compassion as my dad read this account from the Bible. My sister and I began this evening ritual on the nights we stayed with my dad twice a week. I was ten years old, and my sister was seven.

"Yes, we will read the story about the one leper who turned back and thanked Jesus when he was healed," my dad answered.

"I really like that one!" I exclaimed.

Jennifer agreed, and we both scurried under the covers to listen to the story that always touched my heart.

At the time, I wasn't sure why this particular story impacted me so much, but I smiled and listened to our dad's soothing voice as he read this touching story about Jesus. In these quiet moments, I felt my dad's love and the security it brought me. Just as he opened the big, blue book to my favorite story, I basked in the

8

safety his presence provided me, and I rested in his love. My ears were open, and my heart was ready to listen to this story. My dad directed us to the gospel of Luke, Chapter 17:11-19, which was one of the miracles Jesus performed for those who were sick.

"Would all of them be healed?" I wondered.

I certainly hoped so.

The Story of the Ten Lepers
An Encounter with Jesus

"Ten lepers had an encounter with Jesus." Our dad began.

"What is an encounter?" I asked.

"An unexpected meeting with someone," he explained.

"Like when I see a good friend of mine at the playground at the park on the same day I'm there?" Jennifer asked.

"Exactly. That's a great example of an encounter."

I thought this over and remembered a possible encounter I'd experienced. "Sally was at the Six Flags last week when we were there. Remember, Daddy?" I asked. "We didn't know each other would be there, so I had an *encounter* with her. That's cool!"

"You're right, Jill, another great example. You did have an encounter with Sally. Let's keep reading so we can see where Jesus encounters these lepers. Remember that these people were isolated from everyone else because of the condition of their skin," Daddy continued.

"Why?" I asked. I knew my dad would know the answer, and because he was a doctor, I respected his insight and opinion.

"Well, this disease of the skin was life-threatening. And if they touched you, it was highly contagious. It could spread by just a small touch. People were afraid of them and wanted to be as far away from them as possible. It was hard to be a leper."

"Have you ever seen these skin spots on any of your patients, Daddy?" I asked.

"No, honey," he answered.

"Are they like cooties?" Jennifer asked. The word 'cooties' made us laugh, but only because we didn't understand the gravity of leprosy.

"It was not a laughing matter," Daddy continued with compassion in his gaze. "These people were made fun of and thought to be unclean. Because of this, they felt extremely lonely." As a doctor, I knew this touched my dad's heart, and I could see the sympathy in his teary eyes. His response, along with the words of the story, touched my heart as well, and I felt the tears flow down my cheeks.

"Did Jesus touch these lepers, or was he afraid like everyone else?" I asked.

"The lepers stood at a distance when Jesus approached their village, but they lifted up their voices and said, *'Jesus, Master, have mercy on us.'* When Jesus saw them, he was not afraid, but told them to go show themselves to the priests," Daddy explained.

"Why did they need to go to the priests, Daddy?" my sister questioned.

"Well, they needed to be cleansed from the disease by the priests. This is what the law said at this time."

"Well, they better follow the law then!" I exclaimed with authority. As the oldest, I was a rule follower and a tattletale for those who weren't. In fact, I had tattled on my sister and her friend when they painted on the entrance wall to our apartment complex. Though she forgave me later, she was furious with me that day for telling on her. "I understand following the rules, Daddy, but what is mercy?" I asked curiously, unfamiliar with the term.

"Good question, Jill, and I am glad you asked. Mercy is forgiveness and compassion for someone who does not deserve it given by someone who could withhold it if they wanted to," Daddy clarified.

"Like when Molly stole the Twinkies out of my lunch, and I forgave her anyways?" asked Jennifer.

"Yes, that would be an example of mercy, Jennifer. And extended mercy was when you still forgave her after she confessed that she had been taking them for several weeks. You gave her mercy when you didn't have to. But here, the ten lepers needed to obey Jesus by going to the priests. As they went to see them, they were cleansed." Daddy's hope in teaching us this was to show us we must always follow the law, ask for forgiveness, and never forget to thank those who offer forgiveness and mercy.

"So, all of them were healed, Daddy?" I asked.

"Well, yes, sort of. They were all cleansed and made well, but they were not all completely healed. Only one leper was made whole." Daddy said.

Jennifer and I, confused, looked at each other. They all obeyed Jesus. They did what He asked. Why was only *one* healed?

"Let me explain," Daddy, reading our puzzled expressions, continued. "Only one leper turned around before the healing and thanked Jesus. He was the one that Jesus touched and made whole in his heart, body, *and* soul. He was not just cleansed, but physically and spiritually healed by his faith and obedience."

"So, the other nine never thanked Jesus?" I asked.

"That is right, Jill. They only did part of what was expected of them."

My heart hurt for the other nine lepers who missed all that Jesus had in store for them. *Was I like them?* I didn't remember thanking Jesus for healing my knee I skinned on my bike accident last week. It could have grown infected, but my dad said a little prayer and it healed quickly. I also forgot to thank Jesus for saving my mother when she was in a severe car accident last month. Her car had been badly damaged, but she came out without a scratch. I felt guilty as I wondered why I never thought to thank Jesus. *Was He waiting for me to thank Him?* I didn't feel right not thanking Jesus, and I wondered if Jesus forgave me for this oversight. I looked up at my dad and asked, "Daddy, does Jesus forgive me for not thanking him when He healed me or saved Mom? I never thought to thank Him."

"Yes, Jill. Jesus forgives you, because he loves you. He died on the cross for your sins. He will always love you."

Something still didn't feel right in my heart and I knew something was missing in my life. I felt lonely and insecure about a lot of things. I wanted to be like the one leper in this story who was healed inside and out. I contemplated, but still couldn't understand. I didn't like the feeling of having the darkness of sin lingering in my heart. Maybe I needed a touch of Jesus in *my* life. I wanted an encounter with Jesus like the healed leper. I needed a friend to listen to me. I wanted a friendship with Jesus, knowing he was the best listener I could ever find. I knew he'd never leave me, and he'd always listen to me. I realized I had been standing at a distance like the other lepers and that I wanted, and needed, to know more about Jesus. Maybe I could learn more from another story tomorrow night. I was growing tired, a little sad, and confused. I knew I didn't have the touch of Jesus on my heart. But now, I knew I wanted it.

Questions raced through my mind.

Did Jesus really love me?

Did He love me when I didn't even know him as my friend?

Did I pray to Jesus so He would know what was on my heart?

Somehow, I knew the answer to all these questions was yes. My dad had told me so. And the Bible told me so. I felt loved. This thought made me smile, and I drifted off to sleep easily as my head hit my soft, pink, polka dot pillow.

In the Dark

I was terrified of the dark. I was also scared of thunderstorms. I will never forget the night I couldn't see. A strong hail and thunderstorm hit our apartment one night and my bedroom window shattered. As the storm raged, all I could do was call out for help. "Mommy! My window is broken! The storm is coming into my room! Where are you? I'm scared!" I cried and violently shook in fear. "I can't see!"

"I'm right here, Jill. Can you hear my voice?"

"I can hear you, but I can't see you!"

As the storm rolled in, the lights in our apartment, with no warning, suddenly vanished. "You can't see me, but you can follow my voice," my mom coaxed.

"I'll try," I whimpered. "but I can't see you." My fear of the dark, coupled with my fear of thunderstorms, left me paralyzed.

"Do not be afraid, I am right here with you," she assured. As she spoke, I remembered the story about the blind man my dad had read to us the other night before bed.

The story was found in the Gospel of Luke. There was a man who couldn't see. His vision had been lost and he was blind. But when he heard the voice of Jesus, he wanted to be healed and to see again.

"I sure wish the lights would come on, right now!"

"Follow my voice, Jill! Do not be afraid." Mommy called.

I was ten years old. I thought I knew everything. But when crippled by fear, all I wanted was to follow my mom's voice and find her. I had to listen carefully to find her. The closer I drew towards her, my fears began to vanish. Finally, I found her and jumped into her arms. I may have felt like a know-it-all, but I did know one thing: I wasn't too old for hugs. In fact, I loved hugs. The touch of those who loved me was like food to my soul. I liked to close my eyes and soak in and feel the touch of love. As my mother hugged me, my heart warmed, and peace flooded through me. I was so glad that she reached for me and that I had found her. I could see again, even in the dark, as I embraced my mother and her love for me. I wondered if the blind man felt the touch of Jesus before his eyes were fully opened.

Did he lose his hope when he lost his sight?

Or did he keep the faith knowing he was loved?

I was going to ask my dad to read the story to me again. I needed to ask more questions. I needed to listen better than I did the previous time he read it. Instead of my crush, Robbie, being on my mind and the great plan my friend, Sara, and I had of telling him of my feelings, I wanted, and needed to hear the story of the blind man. The story hadn't meant much to me until I couldn't see in the dark. I felt lost, confused, and scared. I'd always taken my sight for granted, never realizing I still needed Jesus' help to truly see. *Maybe I should start asking Jesus for help,* I thought.

I could not wait to hear the familiar words from my dad when we would be spending the next night at his house, "Your milk with ice is ready. Drink up and let's get ready for bed, so I can read you another story."

I smiled, knowing exactly which story I needed to hear. I could see again. The lights were back on in our house and in my heart. I was ready to *see*. This time I would stop listening to the other voices in my head. I'd stop thinking about Robbie and upcoming school dances. I'd focus and listen to the story of Jesus healing the blind man on the road to Jericho from Luke Chapter 18:35-43.

God grabbed my attention when the electricity went out. I would listen intently, now, to see if there was a message in the story for me. I was ten and knew most things, but I finally realized I didn't know *everything*. I yearned to know more about Jesus. This Jesus, the Savior, who could save and heal me.

What Do You Want Me To Do For You?

"Daddy read us the story about the blind man, pretty please!" I begged.

"You read that one to us last time, and I want to hear a different one," Jennifer chimed in. "We always do what you want to do, Jill, and it is my turn to pick!"

"Remember when the power went out last night, and we couldn't see? Do you remember the storm? Remember the hail?" Excitement laced my voice as I continued. "I thought about this story and wanted to pay closer attention to what Jesus asked the blind man when he met him on the road."

"Well, I guess I need to listen to this story again too." Jennifer agreed and our dad began reading out of the comforting big, blue Bible storybook.

"In Luke, Chapter 18 in the Bible, this story is found," my dad shared. "Jesus was passing on the road to Jericho when a crowd of people approached Him.

There were many there who had come to see Him because they wanted to meet Him. A blind man was sitting on the ground, on a mat, begging as the people passed him by. The man asked why everyone was gathered and rushing around."

"Daddy, do you think the man was scared because he couldn't see?" I asked.

"I bet he was afraid they might run over him." Jennifer added.

"Yes, girls, I imagine he was a little afraid. But when the crowd told him that Jesus of Nazareth was passing by, he knew that it was an opportunity for him to speak out and seek help because he wanted to recover his sight again."

"Jesus helped him, right?" I asked.

"Let's read more of the story and see what happened." Our dad kept reading, "So as Jesus passed by, the blind man spoke to him *'Jesus, Son of David, have mercy on me!'* But those in front of him told the man to be quiet and stop asking for help. They tried to make him stop. But the blind man spoke even louder saying again, *'Son of David, have mercy on me!'.*"

"There is that word mercy again," Jennifer noticed. People must all need mercy."

"Yes, you're right, Jennifer, *all* people need mercy. And that is why Jesus has come. He wants to give us all mercy," Daddy explained. "even when we do not deserve it. And none of us deserve it."

After my dad said this, something inside of me knew I wanted mercy too. I knew I didn't always do what was right. In fact, the other day, I remembered I had lied to my mom. I hoped Jesus would give me mercy. Maybe I needed to shout out like this man to get his attention. *Surely, He would hear me*, I thought.

Should I ask Jesus for mercy?

I didn't know how to ask.

Did I just shout it out?

Did I tell someone else to tell Him?

I asked my dad, "Daddy, I want mercy like this blind man. I need forgiveness for things I have done. How do I ask Jesus?"

"Jesus wants us to ask Him for what we need. We do this by simply asking like you would ask me for something," he explained. "You can pray to Jesus and ask Him for mercy. He will hear your prayers too." He turned the page. "Let's keep reading to see if Jesus heard this man. As soon as Jesus heard the man, He stopped and commanded the people to bring the man to Him. When he came near, He asked the blind man, *'What do you want me to do for you?'* And the man said *'Lord, let me recover my sight!'*."

"Oh, I see. Jesus wants to know what we want when we call upon Him." Jennifer's face brightened at her discovery.

"Yes, Jennifer, that is obvious. Of course, Jesus wants to know what we want," I replied in my strongest Miss-Know-It-All voice. After I said it, I realized I, myself, hadn't been asking Jesus for anything, not even for a little help. I was doing everything without Him. I rarely prayed, and even then, only the bedtime prayer beginning with the words, *"Now I lay me down to sleep."* But even in those moments, I didn't feel like I was talking to Jesus. My heart sank as I realized I didn't know how to talk to Jesus. *Would he forgive me?*

"Did Jesus give the man his sight back?" I asked.

"Well let's read on and see what happened," Dad said. "Jesus said to him, *'Recover your sight; your faith has made you well.'* The answer is right there, Jill. He did get his sight back because Jesus healed him immediately."

"That is so amazing!" I shouted.

"I'm glad he got his sight back!" Jennifer exclaimed.

"What did he do next?" I asked.

"Well, after his sight was recovered, he followed Jesus, glorified God, and all the people who saw it gave praise to God." Daddy said.

"So, he didn't just go about his business getting what he wanted?" I asked.

"No, Jill. This man followed Jesus. He wanted to do what Jesus wanted him to do, and he glorified God for this miracle."

"What does glorifying God mean?" Jennifer asked.

"It means that he was thanking the Lord and giving Him all the credit for the healing. He realized that it was only through Jesus that he was made well. It was not anything he did himself, but through God. He also wanted others to know that God had healed him so that they would believe too. This man's faith led others to give thanks and believe in the Lord."

Daddy seemed excited as he shared these truths with us. His face lit up with joy as he read from the pages. He shared hope with us, and I knew why I had wanted him to read it again. I needed to hear that Jesus wanted to know what I needed and that I could ask him. I needed to pray. I needed to be still so I could focus, learn, and know Jesus. I wanted his mercy. I decided I would ask him before I fell asleep.

Would He hear me?

I sure hoped so.

As I was thinking about what I would tell Jesus, I heard a still, small voice inside my head ask me, '*What do you want me to do for you?*'.

I wanted a touch of Jesus on my heart.

I knew He wanted to give me what my heart desired, but I needed to ask.

After my dad tucked me into bed, I closed my eyes and said a little prayer for Jesus to come and reach me because I was lost and wanted to be found.

What Do You Do If You Have Not Felt the Touch of Jesus in Your Life?

I realize today that those nights with my dad reading me bedtime Bible stories formed the beginnings of who I am today in Jesus Christ. Jesus *did* hear me and *did* love me just like He loved all those who He encountered on the pages of the blue, Bible storybook. The very questions I had as a child were answered in the words from the Bible. The seeds of love were planted within me so that they would grow, and I would someday invite Jesus into my heart and accept His touch upon my life.

The lessons found in each story of the Bible where Jesus encountered people have given me new direction and greater hope today as I reread them with fresh eyes and a renewed heart. I know that Jesus wanted me to know Him. He reached for me early in my life, but I *chose* a different path for the first seventeen years of my life.

"For I know the plans I have for you, declares the LORD, plans for welfare and not for evil, to give you a future and a hope."
Jeremiah 29:11

Many of us have heard the truth as a child, young adult, or older adult but have made the choice to live by our own will. We don't ask Jesus to help us. It is a sad choice Jesus hopes we do not make. He wants us to choose the narrow path, through Him, that leads to life. But the gate is narrow and many do not take it.

"Enter by the narrow gate. For the gate is wide and the way is easy that leads to destruction, and those who enter by it are many. For the gate is narrow and the way is hard that leads to life, and those who find it are few."
Matthew 7:13-14

It is easier to live in our own selfish ways without a care about how Jesus wants us to live. That's how I was living. It is harder to be one of the few and find our security in Jesus alone. I realize now that I was insecure because my security was not in Jesus. I thought I could rely on others for approval instead of wanting to please the one who loved me the most. It is not that my early years were not good or that I was not happy, but there was an emptiness and a hole that could not be filled with anyone or anything. The truth and fullness I was seeking was found in Jesus Christ. Looking back, I know people, like my father and grandmother, were praying for me to find the truth so that the truth could set me free.

"And you will know the truth, and the truth will set you free."
John 8:32

Are you searching for the truth like I was years ago?

Is there someone in your life now or from your past that has been trying to get your attention?

There *is* someone in your life who has prayed for you to find Jesus!

Jesus, Himself, has prayed for you to find Him when you were a little child, and He is still praying for you today. He wants all His children to come to Him. You are His child.

"But Jesus said, 'Let the little children come to me, and do not hinder them, for to such belongs the kingdom of heaven'."
Matthew 19:14

As He prayed, Jesus often went to private places to pray alone to the Father for things that were on His heart. He spent time on His knees and on His face pleading with His Father to save His people. He has prayed for you to have faith and believe, just like He prayed for His disciples who were close to Him. He hopes that everyone will put aside their selfish ways to serve, give, and love others. He gives us a new commandment to love Him and love others as He loves each of us dearly.

"A new commandment I give to you, that you love one another; just as I have loved you, you also are to love one another."
John 13:34

He prays to the Father for all of His people in John 17. He prays out of the love that He has for us, *"I am praying for them. I am not praying for the world but for those whom you have given me, for they are yours." John 17:9*

He wanted us to be set apart and set free with the truth of His Word as He prays to the Father, *"Sanctify them in the truth; your word is truth." John 17:17*

I know the truth now that Jesus loves me and that He hears me when I pray. He has forgiven me for all of my sins from the past. He has forgiven you and wants to have a relationship with you. There is nothing you can do to make Him love you less. He loves you just the way you are, right where you are. His reach is far and wide to all who want to know His love and grace. His grace is enough for all who have sinned and fallen short.

"For all have sinned and fall short of the glory of God."
Romans 3:23

God loved us so much that He gave His only son to us as a sacrifice for our sins. He wants all to lay aside their burdens and come to Him for salvation. Jesus will give you eternal life if you choose Him. Reach out to Him and touch His love for you.

"For God so loved the world, that he gave his only Son, that whoever believes in him should not perish but have eternal life."
John 3:16

If you still have questions, maybe it is time to listen and hear God calling you for that *first touch* upon your heart. He is calling you by name. Believe that He loves you and ask Him into your heart so He can touch you for the first time and change your life. Maybe it is time to be still and listen. God is calling you, just as He was calling me years ago.

Come to the one who knows everything about you and still loves you. Let Him touch you. Keep reading the next section of this book to see how I made the most important decision of my life. You, too, can make the most important decision of your life: to trust Jesus and allow His *first touch* upon your heart!

Jesus has been right there from the very beginning holding all things together. He wants to hold you too. It is time to believe in His promises.

"He is the image of the invisible God, the firstborn of all creation. For by him all things were created, in heaven and on earth, visible and invisible, whether thrones or dominions or rulers or authorities-all things were created through him and for him. And he is before all things, and in him all things hold together."
Colossians 1:15-17

HIS RESCUE

Jill Lowry

My Rescue Story

Inviting Jesus into my Heart

Whoever said being a teenager was not easy, was correct. Not only do we feel awkward in our own skin—because we are leaving childhood and beginning to find our place in the world— But also it is hard to find who we are in Christ if we have not grabbed hold of Jesus from the beginning and let Him rescue us. I was one of those awkward teenagers, searching far and wide to find my confidence and security. I knew there was something missing from my life, but I did not discover that Jesus would stand in the gap for me until after high school. I was searching everywhere else in this world to find hope, simply because I did not know the truth of the power of Jesus. I needed rescuing, in a big way, from peer pressure, self-doubt, and selfishness, but I was too wrapped up in my own life and problems. Those years where I lived without Jesus and His guidance, impacted me for years to come. But now I know that Jesus was right there reaching for me to fall into His arms of grace. He would catch me right where I was if I would open my eyes to see His light and open my heart to touch Him for the first time. He wanted me to open the eyes of my heart!

"Having the eyes of your hearts enlightened, that you may know what is the hope to which he has called you, what are the riches of his glorious inheritance in the saints."
Ephesians 1:18

I was fortunate to have friends and family in my life who directed me to Jesus. But because I was so hardheaded and stubborn at times, it took me awhile to discover the truth. Looking back, I was blinded by my own self-interests and insecurities in those years. Having a lot of friends and pleasing others to get their approval was more important to me than the approval of Jesus. I was like most teenagers my age, striving to be popular in those years before high school. I even tried to be a cheerleader in 7th grade to fit in and fill a void in my life, thinking that this would bring me happiness, but I did not make the squad. With dashed hopes, I drew farther away from the reach of Jesus and kept searching for the happiness I longed for in my friends. I expected them to meet all my needs, which wasn't possible. And I felt like something was missing, even though I had many friends and a family who loved me.

"For am I now seeking the approval of man or of God? Or am I trying to please man? If I were still trying to please man, I would not be a servant of Christ."
Galatians 1:10

One thing that I did have, was my baby blue diary with a lock and my favorite dog, a white poodle, on the cover. I would find comfort from pouring out my feelings on the pages of this cherished diary that my mother gave me for my birthday. I felt refreshed as I wrote my thoughts, dreams, hopes, and desires on each page. I also felt peace when I could express my hurts, heartaches and frustrations on the pages stained with my tears. It was so good to write down my plans and goals, but mostly, that diary became a dear friend to me. As I wrote each word, I felt like I could hear a response of comfort, hope, and love. It was a blessing to be able to be still and share my thoughts on the pages. It was calming to my soul writing down my feelings and sharing my heart. I was waiting for a response from someone who could rescue me. *Could it be I was writing to Jesus but didn't even realize it?*

"Be still and know that I am God..."
Psalm 46:10

I know now that Jesus was speaking to me as I was writing each page, trying to get my attention so that He could rescue me. Journaling in my diary was the time I could be still and find comfort as I poured out my heart. This dear diary became my connection to Jesus even though I had not invited Him to live inside my heart. It was like I was talking to Jesus Himself but did not realize it at the time. As I started each page with *'Dear Diary'*, I knew that my Savior put His name in its place and listened to me like no one else ever could or would! I will open my diary pages to you and let them come to life as I share my love story with Jesus during the middle years of my life. *This* was the moment I finally answered the call to have it all! This is my rescue love story.

"Love never ends..."
1 Corinthians 13:8

The Bold and the Beautiful

Dear Diary,

It is the night before cheerleading tryouts and I am super excited and nervous about trying out! Cheryl, one of my best friends, said that she thought they'd only pick twelve girls from our seventh grade class. I'm confident I will be one of them. My mom told me I am beautiful, and I know I am loud, so I bet I can make the team. I can't wait to cheer for the football players, especially Robbie. Diary, I've had a crush on him since fourth grade. I love his freckles and dark brown hair. He is so cute!

The team captain for the eighth grade cheerleaders, Cindi, taught us the routine a few days ago. It is kind of hard, but I think I can do it. I get nervous performing in front of others, except for my mom, who asks me to practice in front of her. She was a cheerleader for the Kilgore Bulldogs when she was in school. She always gives me good feedback. Then she reminds me, "Smile, Jill, and be bold and beautiful!" My mom is so pretty, too. I think of her as bold and beautiful. I wish I looked more like my mom. Everyone thinks my sister favors her more, but I see myself in my mom's eyes.

My grandpa always tells me how I look like my grandma and that she was so pretty and sweet. He told me that she was one of the first Kilgore Rangerettes when they first began years ago. My dad took us to a show where they performed, and I loved watching them do the high-kicks on the line. I think I like that more than cheerleading, but for now, I will try out because it is the popular thing to do. Sports are not my thing. I am not good enough at volleyball, and I don't like basketball (probably because I'm not very good). Anyways, I will remember to be *"bold and beautiful"* when I try out. I guess that means I need to smile more and yell louder. We will see how I do after school tomorrow. I am getting more nervous by the minute. I feel my mom will be disappointed if I do not make it. And I will not be in the popular crowd if I don't. I'm not sure which I'm more nervous about.

And also, Diary, I am so mad at Tammy because I heard today that Robbie likes her and asked her to go steady. My heart hurts just thinking about her getting to hold his hand. And would he kiss her? I have never kissed a boy. My stomach hurts just thinking about it. Tammy knows I like him, and we are friends. I am not her friend anymore, because right now I am so mad and will never be able to forgive her. I hope she doesn't make cheerleader. She doesn't deserve it. I feel bad saying this, Diary, but you understand. I can't tell anyone else but you. It feels good to get this off my chest. She told me that she'd never go with him if he asked her. We promised each other that we would never put a boy before our friendship. Best friends forever (BFF)— That is what we said. I told her that I wouldn't go out with her crush, John, if he asked me. And when he did, I said no. I'm in shock because she lied to me and said yes to my forever crush. How can a friend do that? Especially a *best friend*. Well, we aren't speaking right now and that is how it is going to be. Cheryl told me yesterday that she saw them holding hands after school. My heart sank in my chest as I heard the terrible news. In fact, I had to go to the bathroom and cry. It hurts so bad! I thought I could depend on and trust my friends. I guess I was wrong. I'm glad I can trust you, Diary. You know my thoughts before I even know them. I'll touch base with you tomorrow and let you know if I make the team. I'm so mad I can't even think about tryouts right now. All I can think about is how Robbie likes Tammy and not me. Life isn't fair. I bet I won't even make the team and she will. That'd be just my luck.

Oh, and I made a bad grade on my English paper because I couldn't focus! I'm worried Mom is going to ground me. Nothing is going right for me right now, but at least my dog, a poodle named Mandy, loves me and won't be mad at me. She's right beside me right now as I write tonight. I'm so glad I have her. She loves me no matter what I do. I don't know what I would do without my puppy dog.

Goodnight, Diary!

♥

I desperately needed a friend at that moment. And if Jesus had written me back that day, I believe He would have answered in this way:

My Dearest Beloved,

I love you. I will never leave or harm you. I will never lie to you. I want you to forgive those who have hurt or disappointed you. If you don't forgive them, you'll only be hurting yourself. Your self-worth is not in which group you belong to but is found in me. You don't need to be in a certain group to be popular, but just be secure in my love for you. My steadfast love endures forever!

*"Give thanks to the God of heaven, for his
steadfast love endures forever."*
Psalm 136:26

If you don't make the cheer squad, I'll provide something better for you. I have a specific plan with your name on it. You don't need to compare yourself with others. I have given you special talents and gifts. Because you haven't invited me to be your friend, you just haven't found all that I want to give you yet. I have a purpose for your life and great works planned for you. Let me begin a good work in you.

"And I am sure of this, that he who began a good work in you will bring it to completion at the day of Jesus Christ."
Philippians 1:6

Your friendships will come and go, but my love for you will *never* fade. In fact, forget about finding security in others and yourself, because I am the one who gives you refuge. Find your refuge *in me.*

"For you have been my refuge, a strong tower against the enemy."
Psalm 61:3

Don't let anyone tell you that you're not good enough. Believe in me and know that my love for you is real. No matter what you have done in the past, I will forgive you and invite you into a relationship with me. There is no other relationship that compares with the one I want to have with you. If you look to me, I will satisfy you, beloved. Come to me, lay all your burdens upon me, and I will give you rest.

Second Touch of Jesus

*"Come to me, all who labor and are heavy
laden, and I will give you rest."*
Matthew 11:28

Your forever friend,

Jesus

I Will Come Back For You

Dear Diary,

Can I say that I'm super mad at what happened Saturday night? I'm not happy with how things turned out when my friend, my sister, and I decided to sneak out of the house. We know it's against my mom's rules. But we sneaked out of the house and toilet papered a friend's house. We just wanted to have fun and some adventure. We can't drive and go do other things since we're only freshmen in high school, so we wanted to do something to have fun. My friend, Stacy, and I wanted to go toilet paper the house of the boy she likes, and my sister asked to come along. She promised not to tell mom if we would let her go. She heard us making plans at dinner, so I agreed to let her come with us. We went to bed and waited until all was quiet in the house. Then, we opened my bedroom window for our escape. I admit, I was kind of scared, but I knew it would be a blast. I just knew we couldn't get caught. Well, as the story unfolds, we did get caught and it was not something I ever want to do ever again. I did not like what happened, and it scared me to death. This is what took place:

Stacy and Scott have always liked each other since the fifth grade. His parents are strict about girls, so he can't ask her to go with him. We thought it would be funny to paper his house so he would know somebody has a crush on him. This is what all our friends are doing, and it is kind of a trend in our class to paper houses of the boys we like. So, we collected toilet paper rolls in my closet for weeks and hatched the plan that we would do this when the time was right. Tonight seemed right, and we had just the right amount of toilet paper to roll his house really great. We were excited! So, when the clock struck midnight, we sneaked out the window of my room.

We escaped without anyone seeing us. It was freeing to leave and head out the door to the neighborhood where Scott lived. The three of us saved our energy by walking to his house. After we arrived, we each grabbed some rolls out of our grocery sacks and threw them high into the tall elm trees in Scott's front yard. It was fun throwing them up into the air, back and forth, until the trees were draped from limb to lawn. I admired our work. But while I stood there liking our excellent wrapping skills, a light suddenly flipped on from the front porch. I heard a dog bark, then the front door opened abruptly. I thought it might be Scott coming out to say hi and laugh at what we had done. He could never be mad at us. But, instead, his dad and brother ran out of the door yelling and cussing at us. They were extremely angry and said, "Whoever this is better come here, or we are calling the cops!" I was terrified.

This was not how we thought things would turn out, so we ran as fast as we could so we would not get caught. I never thought I could run as fast as I did that night. I ran like a scared rabbit, leaping, and bounding, and darting to avoid detection. We were headed back home as fast as we could. I saw Stacy running a little behind me, but she kept pace with me. We were almost there. I didn't see Jennifer near us but assumed she was just a little bit behind us. We got to the house and tried to catch our breath. Thankful that we lost Scott's father and brother somewhere in the neighborhood, I wondered where my sister was. We waited for what seemed forever, and then I started to panic. Where was she? I was in big trouble if something happened to her. I was responsible for getting her involved in this. I told Stacy that she was nowhere in sight and she said not to worry and that we needed to stay put.

I couldn't stay at the house but had to go back to find my little sister. She trusted me to protect her, and I would be letting her and everyone else down if I didn't go back. So, I told Stacy that I was going back to find her. She needed help and I needed to be there for her. Stacy said she wasn't going to leave, and I could go ahead if I wanted. I begged her to come help me, but she said no. Again, another friend who has let me down. I had to go alone, and boy, was I scared. Not only did I not know what happened to Jennifer, but I also had to walk alone in the dark. And we know how I feel about the dark. It was pitch black outside, not even a star in the sky to help shed some light, and I was blocks away from Scott's house. As I ran back, I thought about what I would say to Scott's parents if she got caught. Would I take the blame or let her fend for herself? I wasn't sure but really hoped I could find her. I called her name as I ran. With each step, I felt guiltier and guiltier. I should never have agreed to do this, and I should never have taken Jennifer. She just wanted to be included, and I messed it all up. She always wanted to hang out with my friends and me, and this time, I thought she could help us. *Why do bad things always happen to me?*

She was nowhere to be seen and I started to worry. What if something bad happened to her? What would I do? Could I live with this my whole life? Fear trickled up my spine as I kept calling her name with no response. I wished I had someone to help me. But I knew in my heart, that it was me who needed to go back for her. It was my burden to bear, so I picked up my pace and kept running faster and faster. I hoped she was alright.

As I approached Scott's home, still covered with toilet paper, I saw my sister. She sat in the front yard on the lawn, her knees huddled to her chest. The whole family, including Scott, was out on the lawn looking at her. I couldn't see the expressions on their faces, but their body language looked angry as they threw up their arms when speaking to her. They yelled extremely loud and cursed at her. I could only see Jennifer's back, so I didn't see if she was crying, but she was shaking. My heart sank within my chest. This was all my fault. I should never have disobeyed Mom. I was going to get into big trouble. I failed, again, and I was afraid of what was going to happen.

I took a few deep breaths and walked towards the group, not sure what I planned to say. Maybe they'd forgive us and just let us go. I hoped Scott would defend us since we were friends. All eyes were on me as I walked closer. The look on everyone's face was pure anger and disgust. I knew I'd need to take the blame and apologize for what happened. I'd make the sacrifice to get Jennifer back. I had to. I had to rescue my sister. I had to ask for forgiveness if that is what it took to be forgiven and to get Jennifer back.

Scott's dad spoke first, "Who are you? Were you involved in ruining my yard this evening, young lady?"

"Um, my name is Jill, and yes sir," I said with guilty eyes.

"Do you know this girl we caught running away from our house?" he asked, anger written all over his face. "She said she was with her sister and her friend tonight."

"Yes, sir. I'm her sister, and it was my idea. I'm sorry for the mess we made. Please forgive us and please don't punish her. It's my fault. I'm the one to blame. I can clean it up right now." With dark eyes, he looked back at me. I saw no forgiveness in his gaze. He scared me, because there was only pure hatred in his eyes. I felt an uneasiness that I'd never felt before, as he shined his flashlight in my face.

It seemed like he had no desire to answer me, but his son, Scott's brother, finally spoke up and said, "Oh, Dad, just let them go. I'm sure they didn't mean to harm anyone. This is just a childish prank." Scott stared at me and didn't say a word to defend me. He acted like he didn't even know me. I was shocked because I thought we were good friends. It hurt my feelings and my heart. I just looked at him with sadness and saw no compassion.

Finally, Scott's angry dad said, "I am going to call your mom and dad, young ladies. This was a bad thing you two did tonight and you need to be punished. I also want you to come back early in the morning and clean it up. I'll be waiting for you, but don't expect any help. Give me your phone number and expect me to call in the morning." We said thank you and he let us go. All the way home, neither of us said a word about the encounter with this angry man. We were both so relieved to be free. Jennifer thanked me for rescuing her.

Diary, I've never felt so scared. Not just for myself, but for Jennifer too. I doubt I will ever go toilet-papering again. Thanks for listening to me. I feel better knowing I can tell you everything tonight.

Goodnight, Diary!

♥

If Jesus responded to me during this time of trouble, I believe this is what He would have said to me:

My Dearest Beloved,

First of all, remember that my love for you is everlasting and forgiving. I love you so much that I have forgiven you even when you have been disobedient. I love you so much and will always be with you, even when you feel alone. Do not let your heart be troubled anymore. Come to me, because my love will conquer all your fears. My love endures all things.

"Love bears all things, believes all things, hopes all things, endures all things."
1 Corinthians 13:7

Others may leave you even when they say they love you. You have seen this many times in your life. I came to this world in the flesh so that I could experience this world and walk where you have walked. I know what it is like to be abandoned. I was persecuted, denied, mocked, laughed at, and left out just like you have been. I also know the sin you have been seeing in this world. I know the temptations you face. I see the hurt in your eyes. I have compassion for you, Jill. I dwell among you and want to dwell in you. Do you see me? I am right here beside you. I want you to see my glory from the Father who is full of grace and truth.

"And the Word became flesh and dwelt among us,
and we have seen his glory, glory as of the only Son

from the Father, full of grace and truth."
John 1:14

I came into this world to live and die just to save you! Through my death, you can be set free from sin. In this world, you will have troubles, but in me, you will be set free. Where the Spirit of the Lord is, there is freedom! I suffered so that you could be set free! I took your burdens so I could rescue you for eternity. You took all the blame for your actions so that you could rescue your little sister. And just like you took the guilt for your sister and rescued her, I have rescued you, but my rescuing is for eternity! I suffered it all on the cross, so that my blood could wash over you and save you forever! In me, you have eternal life!

"Since, therefore, we have now been justified by his blood, how much more shall we be saved by him from the wrath of God."
Romans 5:9

You have seen darkness in this world. The hearts of my people have grown dull. Many do not yet see because they do not believe. Their eyes are evil and full of hatred. They are not sorry and will not take the blame for their actions. But do not lose heart, my precious child, for I am the way in the darkness. You see, when you believe in me, you are no longer alone, for I will be with you inside your heart. I will be the light within you. A light in this dark world. I came to bring the light to the darkness and truth where there was none. The way to the truth and life is through me.

"Jesus said to him, 'I am the way, and the truth, and the life. No one comes to the Father except through me.' "
John 14:6

Believe in me, Jill. I am the one who will give you all that you have been searching for. Trust me with all your heart. You may not understand, but keep your eyes on me, invite me to live in your heart, and you will have eternal life! Confess with your mouth and believe in your heart that God raised me from the dead and you will be saved once and for all! Tell me that you love me and want me to live in you. I love you, Jill. Now, take my hand and let me walk with you in every decision or challenge you face. With me, you will not have to go alone or face your fears by yourself. I will never let you down. I am with you, until the end of the age. Confess and believe!

"Because if you confess with your mouth that Jesus is Lord and believe in your heart that God raised him from the dead, you will be saved. For with the heart one believes and is justified, and with the mouth one confesses and is saved."
Romans 10:9-10

Your Savior,

Jesus

Through the Fire

Dear Diary,

This week has been one of the hardest for me in my high school years but has also been one of the most miraculous. In fact, it has been a desperate time for my friends and me. I'm so sad about the tragic loss of a dear friend in a car accident last weekend. I still can't believe that John is gone! He was one of the sweetest and funniest people in our school. And my friend, Mary, is devastated because she just lost her boyfriend. I have tried to console her, but don't know what to say. She's completely crushed and so am I. It seems like a nightmare for those of us that were with him the night he died. We've cried so much I feel drained of all my energy. And I'm confused. Confused and sad as to why someone so loving could die so young. He was only seventeen. We were celebrating his birthday, and I don't think I will ever understand why this happened on that particular night. He's the first person my age that I've known well that has died. His death has touched something deep in my soul, Diary. I've never been to a funeral before today. My friends and I went to say goodbye to John, and I'm still not over it.

I have to tell you about the horrible night. I *have* to write it all out. Maybe then I'll understand. Maybe then I'll know why John had to die. Our school has changed. I wish I could say it has changed with John still here, but his death has sparked something different in the school. It's brought us all closer together, as if we now realize that life is short and precious. We all united our hearts and a miracle happened. I have to write this, diary, because I need to get it all off my chest after the funeral, and I know I will never want to forget how we all changed that day. I haven't shared my feelings with anyone, and I'm heartbroken.

It all started on Friday night. A group of us wanted to go to our favorite Mexican restaurant downtown, Mi Tierra, to celebrate John's seventeenth birthday. We made big plans a few weeks ago because we wanted to make it special for him. John was one of those people who made everyone laugh and feel good about themselves. All who knew him were blessed to call him their friend. I was one of those lucky people.

There were twelve of us who decided to go that rainy, foggy night. My dad didn't like the idea of me going, but I insisted I needed to. "I'll be safe," I assured him. We were driving in two cars to the restaurant which was about thirty minutes from our neighborhood. I was excited to celebrate a friend's birthday! We couldn't wait to all spend time together and we just knew it would be fun. We had great plans for the best birthday celebration ever!

I still remember every detail from that night. The laughter was contagious when John was around. As usual, we laughed at all his jokes. The stories he told made us feel at ease and in a good mood. I just loved being a part of this fun group and was glad I was invited. And Mary made sure I'd be there because we were best friends.

Well, after the meal, we all agreed to go back to the parking lot behind Jack in the Box in our neighborhood, our hang out, and talk more. I didn't want the evening to end! I was in one car with Debbie, Sara, Jack, Steve, and Cindy. The car in front of us was loaded up with Mary, John, Lonnie, Jane, Karen, and

Patti. Jack was driving our car and Lonnie was driving the other car. As most boys like to do, Lonnie and Jack decided to race each other on the way home. As we merged onto the interstate, we picked up speed and drove way too fast. It was all in fun. It felt great to laugh with friends and have a little competition. But the faster we went, my stomach started feeling queasy and a bad feeling crept over me. I wanted the boys to slow down but I did not want to say anything from the back seat. I just hoped we would get there soon.

The car John and Mary were riding in zoomed in front of us and before I knew it, I saw it spin out of control on the slick roadway and hit the embankment on the side. We all grew quiet, terrified at what we just witnessed and hoped our friends were okay. But then the car burst into flames. I started screaming, "Help! The car is on fire!" I couldn't believe my eyes. We slowed down but had to keep going until we got to the next exit to get help at the Stop-N-Go convenience store. The employee called the police and ambulance for us as we described the location. It seemed like a bad dream and all of us were in shock. I have never been so scared in my life. We drove back to the location and saw that the car had exploded, and the first responders were already there trying to rescue our friends. I couldn't see who all came out of the flames, but continued counting heads, hoping to see all six of my friends walk out of the car. I saw Lonnie, the driver, but that was it. My best friend, Mary, was nowhere to be seen and I couldn't see John. I was so worried about all of them. The police wouldn't let us get close to the car and told us to go home. We traveled home in complete silence all trying to process our shock of the situation. I'm still surprised we made it home.

When I walked into the house, my mom said she'd already heard what had happened from Mary's mother who'd been contacted by the police. She said Mary was fine but shaken up because one person died in the fire. She didn't know which one. My heart sank as I thought of each of the other five people, their faces, their laughter, haunted in wondering who didn't make it out alive. I laid awake all night re-living the accident and recounting all the events leading up to the fire. I don't know how I'm ever going to get over this, diary. I wish I could talk to Mary.

Saturday morning, my mom came in my room and told me she talked to Mary's mom again and that the person who died was John. He had pulled all the others out of the fire and as he was rescuing Mary, who'd passed out, he caught on fire and died immediately at the scene of the accident. "No! It can't be true! This can't be happening!" I screamed.

"I am so sorry, Jill," she said, walking over to my bed. Wrapping her arms around me, I melted into sobs. I've never felt so weak and helpless. I will miss John so much, and I know Mary is going to have a really hard time.

"Can I see Mary?" I asked. "Where is she?"

"She is already home, but her mom said she has been sleeping for hours and hasn't woken up. This can happen when people are in a state of shock. We can reach out to her tomorrow and maybe go see her then."

I agreed, reluctantly, but knew that things would never be the same at our school. That night changed everything, and I wasn't sure if I wanted to go back.

I didn't see Mary until the funeral today and she looks terrible. Her eyes are red and swollen and wearing new bags underneath them. Her face is sad and she looks as white as a sheet. My heart hurts for her. I wonder when she will ever get back to her normal, cheerful self. I imagine it will take some time. The miracle of life has been overshadowed by the death of her boyfriend. He saved her life! I wonder if she realizes that. I knew the truth. I knew he died because he turned back to rescue everyone else. He risked his life by facing down the flaming vehicle to reach an unconscious Mary. My mom told me not to tell her any of these details. I also saw Lonnie, and he looks wrecked. Wrecked by guilt, I'm sure, since he was the driver. My heart hurts for him. For all of us.

It seemed as if our whole school was at the funeral. I saw teachers and students coming in the doors of the church where John grew up. I'd never been in this church, but there was a welcoming warmth as I walked through the doors into the sanctuary. It felt good to mourn in a place like this with all the people from our school who loved John. I felt a peace there like I'd never felt before, even in the midst of this tragedy. I don't know why, but the church gave me comfort. All eleven of us that were with John the night he died sat together in the front of the church. We held hands and cried as the pastor talked about John and his faith. I had no idea John was close to God. He never talked about his faith to me. The pastor told us that John had accepted Jesus into his heart when he was eight and was in Heaven today. I thought about that and felt even more peace wash over me. Even though I will miss him, I now know he is in a place that is far better. At least, that is what I imagine Heaven to be like.

But during this service, I realized, I don't know much about Heaven at all. What if I had been the one to die that night? Would I go to Heaven? I haven't invited Jesus to live in my heart yet. I don't fully understand everything about Jesus. I know *about* him from when I was little, but I hadn't thought about him in years and knew I didn't have a relationship with Him. At the funeral, I listened to the pastor say, "Jesus wants all of us to come to Him as He invites us to let Him live in our heart. He loves each of you like He loves John and wants a relationship with you. He wants you to believe that He is your Savior so that you can have eternal life." My heart started beating faster as he spoke. I knew I hadn't done that. But I want to know Jesus. I *want* to be in Heaven one day. I want Him in my life and heart. The miracle of life has continued for John somewhere else, in a place called Heaven, where I hoped I would be someday as well. I wanted to see my friend again.

I felt desperate sitting in the pew with my friends. We lost our friend. I remember looking up and seeing John's family who'd lost a son and a brother. They walked to the front of the church and held hands around a portrait of him as a child. Then, the pastor led us all in a prayer called the Lord's Prayer, that admittedly, I didn't know. But as I listened to the words, I knew that something wasn't complete in me. I didn't have a relationship with Jesus. My friend, John, that day in his church, through his life and death, had rescued me by bringing me closer to Jesus. His celebration of life service made me want to celebrate the life I could have in Jesus. I knew I didn't understand everything. I wanted to know more and decided to talk to my dad about what I need to know for Jesus to be my Savior. I wanted to come back to that church with my dad. The Bible stories he read to me as a kid are coming to my mind. I remembered the story of Shadrach, Meshach, and Abednego who were saved from harm in the fiery furnace when an angel of the Lord joined them in the flames. God had sent John to save my friends that night in the fire. He was their angel in the fire! I closed my eyes and prayed believing that there would be a miracle waiting for me in the throes of this desperation and then, as I opened my eyes, I felt a peace settle deep inside my soul that warmed every part of me.

Goodnight, Diary.

♥

At this desperate moment in my life, I believe if Jesus had written back to me, I believe He would have shared these words of hope:

My Dearest Beloved,

I know you are hurting, and you don't fully understand. It is hard when the people we love are hurting. It's even harder when we have to say goodbye, for now, to those we love. I had a hard time leaving my loved ones on earth as I left to be with my Father. But I didn't leave them as orphans. Because I went to be with my Father, you can have a forever friend in the person of the Holy Spirit.

"I will not leave you as orphans; I will come to you."
John 14:18

When you make me Lord of your life, I am with you always in your heart. All you need to do is call upon me as your Lord and Savior, believe in me, and love me with your whole heart. I have given you a heart to love.

"I will give them a heart to know that I am the Lord, and they shall be my people, and I will be their God, for they shall return to me with their whole heart."
Jeremiah 24:7

When you come to me, I will draw near and wipe away your tears. Know that I feel your pain and your heartache, because I'm near to the brokenhearted and I bind up their wounds.

"The Lord is near to the brokenhearted and saves the crushed in spirit."
Psalm 34:18

I suffer when you suffer and weep when you weep. But there is hope for you, Jill. Trust me with your heart, lean not on your own understanding, but lean on me. For if you do, I will show you the path that leads to life and not death. Keep looking up to me and trust me, Jill.

"Trust in the LORD with all your heart, and do not lean on your own understanding. In all your ways acknowledge him, and he will make straight your paths."
Proverbs 3:5-6

Your friend, John, is with me in Heaven. You will see him again if you will make the choice to make me your Lord. He made the choice when he was a young boy to believe that I died for his sins and rose from the grave, conquering death and the consequence of sin. And for all who believe in me, they will inherit my kingdom in Heaven. John was saved, Jill. I forgave him for all his sins, and I will forgive you too, my precious daughter. Confess to me that you need a Savior, trust me with all your heart, and believe that you will be saved.

John is not there with you now, but he is with me. You can be a part of my Kingdom when you say yes to life in Christ. For to live in me is gain because you gain access to my Kingdom with eternal life promised to you in Heaven. It is your choice to make.

"For me, to live is Christ, and to die is gain."
Philippians 1:21

I will live in you, Jill, as you trust me and let me in your heart. You will find a peace like the one you felt when you celebrated John's life. I am your peace. There is life when you come to me just as you are. Pray to me. I will hear you and answer you. You do not have, because you have not asked me. What is on your heart, dear daughter? Do you need a Savior? Are you standing in the need of prayer? If so, let *me* rescue you from the fire. I will walk through the fiery furnace to rescue and deliver you!

"If this be so, our God whom we serve is able to deliver us from the burning fiery furnace, and he will deliver us out of your hand, O king."
Daniel 3:17

I love you. Let me rescue you.

Jesus

Up in the Balcony

Dear Diary,

It's been a few weeks since I've written to you. I've been processing the past few weeks of what has happened in my life. After the accident and funeral for John, we've all been living a bit differently. The things that were so important to us have changed in the blink of an eye. The drama that we usually see at school has died down. It's as if our friend is still with us in spirit and wants us to come together. I think we've all tried just a little harder to be closer to one another. I've even forgiven others who have hurt me. The pain I feel now just makes everything else seem less urgent. I need all my friends, and we need each other now more than ever. I know something inside of me is about to change. I feel a shift in who I am and what I want for the first time in my life.

My friend, Patti, has invited me to her church lately. I never really wanted to go before we lost our friend, but now I've decided to go anytime she asks me. Each time I go, I find myself seeking more of Jesus and who He is, but I'm still so uncertain. I listen intently to the sermon from the preacher hoping that he will share something that will help me. I'm still struggling with the death of John. But to my surprise, his messages of love and hope do help me each time. I still just have so many questions though, and I'm too afraid to ask them.

I didn't grow up going to church every week, but I did attend some Sundays when we went to East Texas to visit my grandparents. I don't know much about the Bible except for some of the Bible stories my dad read to us. My dad also took us a few times to a church near our home, but we didn't join or attend regularly. I've never felt at home at any other church except Patti's. I like spending the night with her on Saturday night so I can go with her family on Sunday mornings. They never miss a Sunday as far as I can tell. She is lucky to have a church to call home, and I wish I could be a part of a church family.

I asked my family about coming with me sometime, and they agreed to go, so we went yesterday. We sat up high in the balcony together and listened to the music and the message of hope. Trinity Baptist Church is a big church with hundreds of people attending each week. I liked sitting up in the balcony where I wouldn't be noticed, yet I could hear and see everything happening below. The music there takes me away to another place: a peaceful place where I can escape my reality. The message yesterday made me think and process things I've never even thought about in my seventeen years on this earth. One thing that stood out to me was the fact I am a sinner, and that God has forgiven me. He has forgiven me for *EVERYTHING*! All those mean things I've said to my family and friends, the times I've disobeyed the rules, the cuss words I have said, and even for the times I took what didn't belong to me... all are forgiven in the eyes of God. But the pastor said that I need to accept Jesus as my Savior to be saved. As I sat in the balcony, I was still unsure how exactly that worked. *How was I to be forgiven? What did I need to do to earn that forgiveness? Or be given that forgiveness?* He said something about deciding to follow Jesus and make Him the Lord of my life. I still felt far away from ever making that decision. I've spent my whole life without Jesus. I thought I would just come and listen in church and not make this decision right now. I like being in the upper balcony where I can hear, but not be seen. I like living at a distance for now. It is comfortable up here, and I can leave the building anytime I want. But, today, as I sat there with my family, I wanted to stay right there and worship because it just felt *right*. I felt a spark of hope touch my heart for the first time and I smiled because my family, who I love dearly, was sitting with me.

Goodnight, Diary.

♥

If Jesus had been sitting with me in that upper balcony at the church, which now I know He was, I believe this is what He would have said to me.

My Dearest Beloved,

I know your heart has been far from me in the past, but through the trials of life you've recently faced, you can find the help you need in me. Sit still, listen, worship, pray, and let me in your heart. Everything you need is found in me, my dear. I will rescue you and take all the pain away. Your pain will turn to joy as you let go and let me take your hand. You don't need to be afraid. I will hold your hand and bring you closer to me.

"For I, the LORD your God, hold your right hand; it is I who say to you. 'Fear not, I am the one who helps you'."
Isaiah 41:13

Do not be afraid, for I am calling you by name. You will hear me when you listen. You are comfortable in this place of worship because I am here with you. I will meet you in the balcony and take you to another place where you can be free of worry, pain, insecurity, abandonment, fear, and disappointment. Open your heart to my love and say yes to me. I want a real relationship with you right *now*. Don't put me off because you're afraid, Jill. You have nothing to fear. You do not have to live alone. I am waiting to welcome you and put my touch upon your heart. It is your choice to make. Open your heart and your soul and make me the Lord of your life!

"But from there you will seek the LORD your God and you will find him, if you search after him with all your heart and with all your soul."
Deuteronomy 4:29

Step out of your seat of comfort and step into a relationship that begins with trust. You can trust me to be with you. I will lead you where you need to go. I will help you in every decision and with every step you need to take even when you don't understand. Your path will be straight when you let me lead you, Jill. Just say yes, and I will "touch" you with the *first touch* of my love upon your heart. I will make you a new creation. It can begin today if you decide to trust me now.

"The LORD is my strength and my shield; in him my heart trusts, and I am helped; my heart exults, and with my song I give thanks to him."
Psalm 28:7

It is time to let go! I love you and will change your life if you say yes to me! I will be with you as you pass through the water and when you walk through the fire. I have called you by name, Jill. You are mine and I can redeem you. I can rescue you.

Second Touch of Jesus

"Fear not, for I have redeemed you; I have called you by name, you are mine."
Isaiah 43:1

I make all things new and can do the same in you! When you are in me, Christ your Savior, the old will pass away, and the new will come! I love you, Jill. Believe that I will rescue you!

"Therefore, if any one is in Christ, he is a new creation. The old has passed away; behold, the new has come."
2 Corinthians 5:17

Come to me,

Jesus

The First Touch of Jesus

His Call Upon My Heart

Dear Diary,

I'm sorry I haven't shared with you much lately. I've been keeping myself busy and just haven't sat down and taken the time to write. But I have to tell you the best news! So much has happened since I last wrote to you, that I can barely contain myself. I finally understand why I was so torn and confused. I finally understand who was pulling on my heart. I've been going to church every Sunday for months now and I've been really trying to listen with my heart instead of my head. It's a new way of listening, and I find it rather refreshing and rejuvenating to my soul! I feel lighter, happier, and *free*. And I want to write it all down, diary, so that I won't forget. I never want to forget the moment I let Jesus into my life.

The struggle I'd been having because of my sins and insecurities started coming to light the beginning of my last year of high school. Of course it was a big year for me because of graduation, but little did I know that I would make the most important decision of my life. A decision that would completely change my course. It's like I was sailing without an anchor, just floating here and there, without a life preserver all those years before. I've been through multiple life-changing challenges over the course of my life and even several close calls. I almost drowned when I was younger, and that experience, that feeling where my life flashed before my eyes, is still vivid to me. And it wasn't until I surrendered in the struggle and let go that God saved me from drowning. These moments in my life were opportunities or turning points that I let pass me by. Even as the waters raged around me at times, I never found peace. I just drew into myself and was afraid to move in a different direction. But this year, I started listening to a still, small voice, like a gentle whisper, as I would enter the sanctuary of the church. Just as the music started playing inside, the raging waves of anxiety in my mind would calm down and peace would settle over me. I was calm enough to listen. I know now that I needed to be in worship to hear God's voice. And God could rescue me right there as I stepped into the boat with Him instead of drowning outside of the boat with fear and doubt.

I want to share here with you, diary, what happened that December morning in the main part of the sanctuary close to God's love. I finally let God write His love on my heart. After months of attending church from afar in the balcony, I finally decided to move to the lower part of the sanctuary closer to the preacher, the choir, longtime members of the church, and most importantly, closer to God. I'd been afraid to sit close because I didn't want to be noticed. But something inside me knew I needed to listen and see what God had been trying to tell me my entire life. So I took the plunge and switched my seat. After all, I was more mature as a college student. After moving downstairs, I heard the message and the music more clearly and immediately drew closer to God as the hymns touched my soul and the teaching from the Word of God by Reverend Buckner Fanning, spoke to my heart. My eyes and my ears were opened wide, and I felt awakened to what God had been trying to tell me all along: **I was His, and He loved me.**

I remember hearing about how much God loved me no matter what I had done in my past. I started to finally feel a sense of security in that because of His saving grace that He lavishly wanted to pour into my life. This saving grace was mine *in Christ.* I wanted to be made clean and I needed to be forgiven. I wanted to let go of my past and let God in my life by trusting Him to be my Lord and Savior. I needed that touch of Jesus upon my heart.

The song "I Have Decided to Follow Jesus" was the last song we sang each week. The preacher always invited those who wanted to ask Jesus into their hearts to be saved, to come down to the front of the church during that song. I sang it each week with a lump in my throat and my heart pounding in my chest because I *knew* I wanted to be saved. But I was too afraid to go by myself in front of this big congregation. My fear prevented me from doing what I wanted to do. As I remained in my seat, I thought, "I will get up next week." This went on for weeks until one Sunday, I asked myself why my spirit was so unsettled and why I was so afraid. Then, it hit me...I was *ready* in my heart. Jesus would accept me just as I was. I'd been wanting a relationship with Jesus all along but didn't know how or why He would love a sinner like me. I thought I needed to be a better person for Him to love me. And I thought that I didn't know everything I needed to know about Jesus to be saved. All He wanted was my heart so that I could know His love and grace. He suffered and died on the cross to wipe away my sins and was resurrected so that I could have Jesus living inside of me! I didn't need to do anything to earn my salvation. All I needed to do was admit that I was lost and wanted Jesus as my Savior to set me free. Jesus would forgive me as I let Him live in my heart!

With this new revelation, on the Sunday morning before Christmas, I walked down the aisle with my heart on fire and my soul awakened to the new life that was going to be mine in Christ! As the words of the song, "I Have Decided to Follow Jesus," came into my ears, waves of joy flooded my heart! *I was coming home to Christ!*

God's perfect plan unfolded for me. I had decided to follow Jesus on the Sunday morning before Christmas and I was baptized with my sister on Christmas Eve at the special service to celebrate the birth of Christ. I'll always remember my baptism as I celebrate the birth of my Savior. And I will never forget the moment I came up out of the water when I was baptized! I felt free, clean, and secure for the first time ever and pure joy and peace settled inside my heart. Nothing could ever separate me from Christ now! I was born again with new hope and eternal life was mine when I believed and professed my faith! I once was lost, but now I'm found! The *first touch* of Jesus has rescued me, and I realized, with tears in my eyes, that I would see my friend, John, again in Heaven one day. And most importantly, I had a relationship with Jesus Christ, my Savior! **I was born again!**

It is finally well with my soul! I feel a change is coming for me now that I am out of high school. New opportunities await me. I'm now eighteen and have entered into a new season of college life. I'm also a new person in Christ with a new path before me. Thank you for always listening to me!

Goodnight, Diary

♥

I believe Jesus celebrated in this moment with me. And would cheer me on and encourage me with this response after I gave Him my heart!

My Dearest Beloved,

I am so proud of you! You are a special child of the light who has come out of the darkness and into the light of my love! You are special in my eyes. I see promise in you as you walk in My love. Shine My light wherever you go!

"For at one time you were darkness, but now you are light in the Lord. Walk as children of light."
Ephesians 5:8

As you received Me into your heart, you were awakened to new life. You are new in Christ because you have believed. The things that were so important to you will change as you delight in Me and My desires for you. I want what is best for you!

"Delight yourself in the LORD, and he will give you the desires of your heart."
Psalm 37:4

Jill, you went into the water as a sinner, but your sins did not come out with you. You came out clean. I washed away all of your sins! As you were baptized, you were reborn with the power of the Holy Spirit within you. You are now born of the water and the Spirit. You are part of My Kingdom that has no end!

"Jesus answered, 'Truly, truly, I say to you, unless one is born of the water and the Spirit, he cannot enter the kingdom of God'."
John 3:5

I now live inside of you and will guide you into all truth. I will be there for you always. I will never leave or forsake you. I will comfort you and give you strength. My joy is yours, forevermore. It is for freedom that I set you free. Now walk in freedom as My grace has saved you and My Spirit has empowered you!

"For freedom Christ has set us free."
Galatians 5:1

You are loved, Jill. You can be secure in me. You do not need to wonder where you will spend eternity. I have prepared a place for you in Heaven. There is room for you because you have made room for Me in your heart! Peace is inside you and with you always! I love you!

"Because you are precious in my eyes, and honored, and I love you..."
Isaiah 43:4

You are now safe and secure because I have guaranteed an eternal place in Heaven for you with Me! The joy of salvation is yours in Christ! You have a place in My Kingdom in Heaven and until that day when I take you to Myself, I have work for you to do on Earth to fulfill My Kingdom purposes. Let My Spirit come alive inside you!

"And if I go and prepare a place for you, I will come again and will take you to myself, that where I am you may be also."
John 14:3

I love you precious child,

Jesus

Do You Want the First Touch of Jesus on Your Heart?

God wants all of us to make the decision to follow Jesus by our own free will. He has called us all by name because He loves us. When we decide to follow Jesus, we will receive the *first touch* of Jesus on our heart. We are one choice away from having our hearts connected to Jesus through His grace and love. He has been waiting for us to take His hand and step forward with Him. All we need to do is recognize the need for a Savior. Because we have sinned and fallen short of the glory of God, we must confess of our sins, and then believe in our hearts that Jesus died for us to be free.

"For all have sinned and fall short of the glory of God."
Romans 3:23

As we let go and let Jesus in our hearts *and* we believe in Him and His promises to us, He will give us a new and transformed heart and place a new spirit within us. When we confess with our mouth that Jesus is Lord and believe in our hearts that God raised Him from the dead, we will be saved. Christ floods into our hearts and fills our souls with life. All who make the choice to believe will be saved by His grace. He wants all to come to Him and make our home with Him. The decision to give Jesus our hearts is the most important decision in our lives. In Christ, we have the gift of eternal life. Salvation is available to all who repent and believe!

"For the wages of sin is death, but the free gift of God is eternal life in Christ Jesus our Lord."
Romans 6:23

God loves us even while we are still sinners. His proof of that love is found at the cross where Christ, His only Son, died for us. We are set free from sin and death!

"But God shows his love for us in that while we were still sinners, Christ died for us."
Romans 5:8

As we confess with our mouth that Jesus is Lord and believe in our hearts that God raised Him from the dead, we will be saved. Salvation is available to all who trust and believe! So, it is up to us to call upon the name of the Lord and believe. The *first touch* of Jesus begins when we say yes to faith in Him and no to fear.

"Because, if you confess with your mouth that Jesus is Lord and believe in your heart that God raised him from the dead, you will be saved. For with the heart one believes and is justified, and with the mouth one confesses and is saved."
Romans 10:9-10

Once we do this, we become heirs of God and fellow heirs with Christ. We no longer have to live in sin by remaining in the flesh, but we can live by the Spirit who brings life to us. Life in the Spirit is possible as the Spirit of God dwells within us and makes us new. We have the same powerful Spirit living inside of us who raised Jesus from the dead!

"If the Spirit of him who raised Jesus from the dead dwells in you, he who raised Christ Jesus from the dead will also give life to your mortal bodies through his Spirit who dwells in you."
Romans 8:11

Second Touch of Jesus

The first touch of Jesus in our heart makes it possible to receive *the second touch of Jesus*. He touches our hearts first with His love, *the first touch*, and then touches our soul by giving us His Spirit, *the second touch*. The next section of this book will explore *the second touch of Jesus* and how we can actively live today with this touch upon our lives. Keep reading to see how you can activate the Spirit inside of you to experience restoration and renewal in your relationship with Jesus.

Jill Lowry

HIS
restoration

The Restoration of My Heart and Soul Through Jesus Christ Within Me

A Woman After God's Heart

"I want to know more about Jesus," I told my friends as we were watching our young children play at the playground in the park. I had invited Jesus into my heart and was baptized in college, but I was still not completely sure I fully understood all there was to know about God the Father, His Son, Jesus, and the Holy Spirit. My best friend, Maggie, had told me she had grown closer to Jesus when she started attending Bible Studies at her church. I'd been drifting in my walk with the Lord the last several years, and I was eager to renew my relationship with Jesus.

"Come to our new Beth Moore Bible Study about King David that is starting next week," Maggie invited. "We will be studying about David's life and why he was considered a man after God's heart."

I knew I wanted to be a woman who had a heart close to my Lord, so I gave it some thought. I'd been feeling restless to know more. I was quiet about my faith and kind of "spiritually sleepwalking" since becoming a Christian when I was eighteen. I realized that I was never discipled as a new believer in Christ, but I knew God had been working in my life. In fact, I'd recently seen God answer huge prayers my husband and I prayed for years when I finally became pregnant again after several miscarriages. I felt a tug on my heart as I put my hands on my growing belly holding the promise given to me by my loving God. I had a hunger to grow a deeper relationship with the God who had answered our prayers and filled our life with such hope again. My life was blessed by God and I wanted to know Him more intimately. I was living a wonderful life with a husband who loved me dearly, a young son who adored me, and a precious baby on the way; all answered prayers by a loving and faithful God. All blessings from God who still loved me and wanted me to show my love for Him by living devoted Him.

Did I really *know* Him?

Was I *devoted* to God?

Was He my *friend*?

Did I need another *touch* upon my heart?

These questions kept coming to my mind as my Spirit remained unsettled.

"Please consider joining us on Tuesday!" Maggie reiterated. "We would love to have you study the Bible with us. The stories really come to life when you start looking at the people who knew God and had a relationship with Him. David is a great person to start studying first and I know you will love Beth Moore's Bible studies!"

Something inside of me leaped as I thought about this new challenge and opportunity to grow closer to Christ. And Tuesdays were perfect because my son was in pre-school on those days. I didn't hesitate after being asked again and said, "Count me in! I'm looking forward to it!"

Why do I always need to be asked twice before I respond?

I recognized it was fear that always held me up. I decided to conquer my fear though, and I couldn't wait for the Bible study. Tuesday couldn't come soon enough once I made the decision to join the Women's Bible Study at the Fellowship Church. I made sure I had my Bible from college that I had started reading recently. I was glad to be digging into its familiar pages once again. A bookmark from my college days was tucked amongst the pages as well as the highlighted portions from the Bible study sessions I attended while in my sorority, Delta Delta Delta, at The University of Texas. That study had been so long ago, but I still remembered my group leader and how she encouraged us to try to memorize scriptures. I knew a few but wasn't confident about my knowledge. I never really spent time reading and memorizing the scriptures. My Bible had been closed more than opened for years. I hoped they wouldn't call upon me at the new Bible study. I wasn't ready to share about myself or my relationship with Jesus. But my friend, Maggie, assured me that I could just listen if I wanted to be quiet. I was glad about that. I just wanted to learn how to grow closer to Jesus.

"Good Morning, Ladies!" said the Women's Ministry leader. "We are glad that you are all here to start this study that will change your heart and walk with the Lord. King David was a man after God's heart. Let's begin today with a goal to be a woman after God's heart!"

I liked that goal and I hoped I would be different after I completed the study. There was something special about being in a room of women who studied the Word of God together. A sweet spirit was present in this room where we came together as one. About 100 women came to learn more about how we could grow in our faith. This was just what I had needed to grow closer to Jesus in my heart and soul. I'm thankful I said yes and didn't let my fear stop me from growing my faith. Just as I stopped and said a prayer of thanksgiving to God for bringing me there, joy flooded my soul and I felt my baby, a gift from God, move inside of me! My little baby inside my womb jumped for joy and my heart pounded with hope! Right there in that room of women, I rejoiced knowing that something good was going to happen as I opened the pages of my Bible and wrote the words of God on my heart.

Something special happens when you open both your Bible and your heart. I discovered these blessings as I found a place where I could be still to study, open my Bible, and start my daily homework. I escaped to another place with God when I started reading my Bible. My soul was fed and my heart was at peace for the first time in a long time. As I read about David's life, I could hear the voice of God calling me to step out and be brave because His love strengthened me for any challenges that I'd face. I had just been going through the motions over the years and felt like I could use some strength, especially now that I was pregnant.

David's life was proof that God loves us even when we make mistakes. He sinned against a Holy God, but His heart was repentant, and He wasn't afraid to confess His sins. He admitted he was lost without the Spirit of God inside him. God never left him, and I knew that God had never left me even when I kept making mistakes and ignoring the Spirit. Just like David, I was ready to confess my sins again so I could have a heart after God! So, with a repentant heart, I asked Jesus to touch me again with His love and mercy. Right there with my Bible open to the Psalms that David wrote, I asked God to search my heart and renew a right spirit within me. That familiar wave of peace I'd experienced years before when I had decided to follow Jesus, flooded my soul as tears rolled down my cheeks. As I kept reading, I felt the joy of my salvation again with a willing spirit to begin a renewed relationship with my Lord and Savior, Jesus Christ!

"Create in me a clean heart, O God, and renew a right spirit within me. Cast me not away from your presence, and take not your Holy Spirit from me. Restore to me the joy of your salvation, and uphold me with a willing spirit."
Psalm 51:10-12

For Such a Time as This

After my first study about King David, I made Bible study a part of my everyday life. God's Word was food for my soul, and I needed it to grow my faith. My faith journey depended on the study of God's Word, my daily bread. I yearned to know more about God, and I found the answers I was looking for in the pages of my Bible. I also included devotionals to my daily readings that encouraged me and took me to other wonderful passages in the Word. I joined other Bible studies as the years passed and learned more knowledge of the scriptures with each study. I believe my time in these devotionals and Bible studies planted the seeds for the future writing of my own devotionals: <u>Finding Joy in Jesus</u>, <u>Hearts on Fire</u>, and <u>Be Still</u>. I thank God for watering the seeds for me to grow. He's done more in my life than I could ever imagine because I spend time with Him each day. I've grown tremendously in my faith through the diligent study of God's Word, and I hear God's voice in the whispers of my soul like never before. But I still didn't fully understand my path or the direction he wanted for me. Now, there were glimpses of the Holy Spirit in each study I participated in, but His renewed touch upon my heart didn't fully kick in until I deepened my relationship with Him in prayer. I began to pray often for God to move in my life and I believed He would answer my constant prayers. I desired to know my God-given purpose and calling. Prayer connected me to His heart. I prayed for direction and for Him to increase my faith. I knew I was ready to live out my new-found faith and my calling and purpose for Him in my everyday life.

Rejuvenation hit my heart as I kept praying and I was alive with new faith and ready to step out in that faith to go where God wanted to send me. It reminded me of one of my favorite childhood movies, "The Grinch," when his heart grew and grew because he finally decided to get out of his comfort zone and live out the love that was hidden deep within his heart. I was ready to find the joy that I believed was possible through the power of the Holy Spirit that was awakened within me. I had the nudging for months from Him to grow my trust and my obedience. I know now that God gave me a new opportunity to trust Him and grow my faith because my husband and I had been hearing the same promptings to move to the town where he grew up. Our future plan had been to move there after our children graduated from high school. We were hopeful that was God's plan. As we prayed together more and more, God showed us that He wanted us to put our feet to faith and move *before* our planned time. God had a better plan for our family. The call to move came at a time when my husband and I wanted to walk together with the Lord through our faith. The town where God led us became the place where I felt the *second touch* of Jesus.

This wonderful place we made our new home was filled with a multitude of blessings. But in order to receive those blessings, I needed to put my feet to my faith. It was time for me to activate my faith by stepping out with God and trusting Him and the power of Jesus within me. He gave me courage to lead a Bible study in our new hometown where there was a need for a community-wide ladies Bible study. I listened and obeyed what God had called for me to do, but I didn't feel fully equipped. But God was, and He challenged me to take a risk for Him and through my obedience do what He had called me to do. So, I did. For such a time as this, He gave me all that I needed to step into a leadership role with a friend as my partner. Again, another answer to my prayers! I'd wanted to find a ladies group where I could continue in the joy of fellowship that I'd experienced a decade earlier. And God heard my prayers. Not only that, but He challenged me to be a leader instead of a follower.

On the first day of our new community Bible study, He brought various eager women together to study about the life of Esther. We were from different churches, but we had the same eager hearts for Jesus. This was a new season, a new study, but the *same* God. The God who wanted me to stretch my faith without seeing all the details. I was going to step out in obedience, with courage, to help lead women and live out what God had placed on my heart: to unite the ladies in our community for His glory! I was nervous, but excited to begin a new Bible study as I continued on my spiritual journey. I knew the touch of Jesus and did not want to miss what He had for me.

I was thankful I had listened and not given up hope when God winked at me and said, "My daughter, it is time for you to step up and lead a study. I have prepared you for this day. I will provide all that you need. You have come here for such a time as this." These words, *"for such a time as this,"* kept rolling around in my head. I didn't understand what God meant until we opened our Bible to Esther's story and read God's Word about her calling.

"For if you keep silent at this time, relief and deliverance will rise for the Jews from another place, but you and your father's house will perish. And who knows whether you have not come to the kingdom for

such a time as this?"
Esther 4:14

What was my calling?

As I pondered the answer to this question, and was still before God, I felt a new peace come to my soul. I knew God had my whole life in His hands. God knew right where this peace stemmed from. He'd shown me glimpses of it from the beginning when I heard about Jesus while snuggled up next to my Dad listening to bedtime stories. I learned about Jesus' ministry and God used that foundation for now as I was being challenged to begin walking in the Spirit with Him and establishing my own ministry.

He prepared me and equipped me with His confidence a decade before as I studied His living Word with other women, beginning with my first study of King David. He knew I would be open and ready to lead as I stepped into faith and surrendered to His will and purpose for me. In fact, one of the leaders of the Bible study had told me that one day I would lead a Bible study. She encouraged me to prepare as my turn would surely come because she felt God was waiting for me to step out by faith one step at a time. I thought about what she said but didn't believe I would ever be knowledgeable enough to lead. Little did I know that God was preparing me for *His* plan.

I prayed more during this time of waiting and I saw God connect the dots of faith with some plans He'd shown me. I was getting to live out my dreams in this small town where God planted my family and me. I recognized the valleys I would need to go through would take me to the narrow roads that would lead to my destiny. I knew that I had to first, step out of my comfort zone and look to Jesus, the Author of my life and Perfecter of my faith. When I stepped out to lead the Bible study, my passion for learning grew as did my devotion to God. The stories we studied came to life as they jumped off the page and into my heart. I felt compassion for these people in the Bible just as I did when I was a little girl hearing my father read them to me. My heart drew closer to God the Father, His Son, Jesus, and the Holy Spirit as I studied His Word.

God prepared me as I listened to Him and obeyed the promptings of the Holy Spirit. In this season, I listened intently when I prayed. I acted by faith without fear of failure, something completely new for me. As I continued praying, more opportunities to serve and lead for God in my community presented themselves. My purpose was becoming clearer. God was calling me to do my part to bring unity among the churches in my community beginning with the women. Because we all met in Bible study, we were in place to start planning a gathering of women for more spiritual growth.

A group of twelve women began meeting and praying to see what we could do to bring revival to our community. We met weekly to pray and seek God for answers. Then we partnered with another wonderful group of women hoping for the same thing and had a gathering in our community to see what we could do together for God. Our prayers from the heart were answered because we saw the needs in our community with new eyes and sought God for answers. We listened to the Spirit and knew what we would need to do, united by the Spirit, to start revival in our community. We needed to come alongside the youth in our community to serve them and show them the love of

God. We wanted to see God *move* in our community as we came together and believed. As we grew in grace and truth, Jesus touched our hearts, and we felt the Spirit of the Lord join us together. A united spirit of love *revived* us. We were living out our faith together as one body, with one heart and soul, devoted to God through fellowship, prayer, and His Word.

Living out the Word of God with these women changed me. As a beloved child of God with the Spirit inside of me, I felt a revitalized and contagious joy. I realized that God had been wanting me to be devoted to Him with my whole heart all my life. He had plans for me as I kept in step with His Spirit. As I let go and let Him work mightily in and through me, He increased my faith. I could step out of my comfort zone into a place where *only* God could equip me. I had to do my part to trust, obey, and let His Spirit come to life inside of me. As I was drawing closer to God through His Word and prayer, God spoke life to me. I knew I still had growing left to do, but I was eager to grow in grace and knowledge of His truth by studying His Word more and more. I clung to God through His Word as I spent time learning, praying, and worshipping. One of my favorite scriptures from Proverbs, Chapter 3, verses 5 and 6, came to life as I prayed.

"Trust in the LORD with all your heart, do not lean on your own understanding. In all your ways acknowledge him, and he will make straight your paths."
Proverbs 3:5-6

This truth prepared me for what was about to come! I knew I would find my calling and purpose as I kept listening to the promptings of the Spirit of God inside of me. I was right on the path where God wanted me for "such a time as this."

"If we live by the Spirit, let us also keep in step with the Spirit."
Galatians 5:25

"For we are his workmanship, created in Christ Jesus for good works, which God prepared beforehand, that we should walk in them."
Ephesians 2:10

Where the Spirit of the Lord is, There is Freedom

As my study of God's Word increased and my prayer life deepened over the next few years, my heart grew closer to Jesus and the Spirit of the Lord. I discovered where the Spirit of the Lord was, there was a new freedom. In 2014, I began journaling my prayers and my surrender-story of how God was doing something new in me. I used journals to write down my prayers and His answers to those prayers. I believe God used this as preparation that would lead me to my future calling of being an author who points people to His love. Looking back, I see now that as soon as I began journaling, He directed me to my purpose. I was able to write as I let the Holy Spirit guide and direct me. In my book, Prayers from the Heart, I share these prayers and stories about the power of prayer. In addition to the book, I have written the Prayers from the Heart Prayer Journal and the journal, Love Letters to God, where you can journal your prayers and grow your faith as you see answers to your prayers unfold. I have rejuvenated my relationship with Jesus by praying and journaling my prayers.

As I journaled, I also realized that all of my life, I had been missing a *second touch* of Jesus, the sweet surrender to the Holy Spirit. The Holy Spirit had not come to life in me because I was missing the *second touch* of surrender that was necessary to grow in my faith. I needed to set my mind fully on the Spirit to find life and peace. I was not surrendered to the will of the Father and had not yet activated the gift of the Holy Spirit that lived inside me. I had the knowledge of the scriptures but was not living in the power and presence·

of the Holy Spirit. Knowledge without the Holy Spirit was stagnating my growth and faith. I was not living out my faith in the power of the Word of God *and* the Spirit of God. I wanted to experience revival in my heart so that I could go where the Lord called me, but I needed a true personal revival. Where the Spirit of the Lord is, there is truth and freedom. I wanted this, but I had to come to the point of full surrender to finally understand and grasp hold of this freedom.

"For freedom Christ has set us free..."
Galatians 5:1

"Even the Spirit of truth, whom the world cannot receive, because it neither sees him nor knows him. You know him, for he dwells with you and will be in you."
John 14:17

God put mentors and friends in my life in His perfect timing who counseled and talked to me about my spiritual journey. We prayed for each other and our faith grew. We believed God. We knew He wanted more for us. We studied the scriptures about the Holy Spirit and challenged each other to grow closer to Christ. We wanted all that God wanted to give us and knew that we needed to allow the Holy Spirit to do His work in us. Without a total surrender from self, we wouldn't, and couldn't, live out our God-given callings. I'm truly grateful I searched for God with a surrendered heart, because as soon as I did, He opened doors I'd never dreamed could be opened! All this was possible only because the Spirit of the Lord came to life in me!

"Now the Lord is the Spirit, and where the Spirit of the Lord is, there is freedom."
2 Corinthians 3:17

One day in February 2015, just after a friend led me in a prayer for the Holy Spirit to come to life in me, I fell on my knees in prayer with humility and asked for the Holy Spirit to have His way in my life. I was ready to live in the power of the Holy Spirit. I prayed and a new peace covered my entire being. I experienced a refreshment in my soul. I found direction as I reached up to the Lord in prayer for guidance and purpose for my life. I knew that He had the perfect plan for me and that in order to find it, I must trust the Lord completely and surrender *all* to Him. I had some prayers in my heart and soul that God wanted to answer. It was time for me to let go, trust God completely and let God lead me! It's important that we do this, even after we've experienced that *second touch* of Jesus in our lives. We need to surrender to receive direction. A perfect peace that passed all understanding washed over me as I let go. I wanted to live out my faith. It was time and I knew God needed me to be obedient to the promptings of the Holy Spirit for His joy to be in me.

"Until now you have asked nothing in my name. Ask, and you shall receive, that your joy may be full."
John 16:24

As I prayed, the Lord showed me people that needed my prayers, and my heart was burdened for them. I wanted to help and hoped that I could be used by God *"for such a time as this."* God opened my heart to see the struggles some youth in my community were facing. I heard stories that broke my heart, and I couldn't stop thinking about each young person God brought to mind. With each new face, I saw an opportunity to share hope because I knew what a broken family unit looked like myself since my parents divorced when I was five. Divorce had been the part of my past that God wanted to use for His good. I found my present calling when I started reaching out to Him in prayer for a personal revival of my heart. As tears rolled down my cheeks, I realized that God had equipped me with the desire to help His children who needed more hope like I did as a child. My challenging experiences as a child would prepare me to help these young students in my community. I reflected on my past and saw for the first time how God could take my experiences and use them for greater good and His glory! I knelt down and prayed a prayer of thanksgiving for showing me His plan. I felt His peace enter my soul again.

"Now may the God of peace who brought again from the dead our Lord Jesus, the great shepherd of the sheep, by the blood of the eternal covenant, equip you with everything good that you may do his will, working in us that which is pleasing in his sight, through Jesus Christ, to whom be glory forever and ever. Amen"
Hebrews 13:20-21

Confirmation came swiftly. My prayer was answered. I knew I had come to this town *"for such a time as this"* to grow my faith and be a part of revival in my community. The Spirit inside of me would lead, direct, and guide me to do all that God had put in my heart to do. I could live out my faith by working for the Lord. All my tears turned into shouts of joy as I knew what I was to do for the Lord. He would equip me for a special calling to start a program to help mentor and feed students in need so that they could experience personal revival through love. He placed this calling on my heart, activated it with Jesus within me, and I allowed His *second touch* to bring me to surrender. **I was reached, rescued, and restored in Jesus Christ as I let Him have His way in me.** He would grow the fruit needed to help these students as I stayed connected to the Spirit of the Lord. He would equip me as my heart became obedient to His promptings and if I kept walking by the Spirit. He would strengthen me as I let His power work in and through me for His great glory!

"Truly, truly I say to you, whoever believes in me will also do the works that I do; and greater works than these will he do, because I am going to the Father."
John 14:12

"But the Helper, the Holy Spirit, whom the Father will send in my name, he will teach you all things and bring to your remembrance all that I have said to you."
John 14:26

Revival

After I surrendered, something incredible happened to me in the upcoming days. I listened and applied scriptures to my life and heard the voice of the Holy Spirit directing, guiding, and teaching me in a new and wonderful way. My burdens became God's opportunities for me to help those who needed love and support in my own community. Instead of just focusing on my plan, I followed God's, and I stepped forward in faith for what His plan was for me. I continually prayed for revival and God showed me how to move forward. I had a burning desire for a youth gathering for revival, but God was going to open a door for personal revival that He wanted me to experience first. Before He brought this revival to others, I needed to walk through His door of revival in my own heart. I needed to return to Him, wake up spiritually, and obediently follow what God would show me. Then, I could finally experience true restoration. As I prayed for direction, God showed me that the students I was praying for did not just need a one-time gathering for revival, but a weekly mentoring program that could physically, spiritually, and mentally feed these students in need. They needed to be encouraged along the way and mentored continually with a weekly outreach program. This would bring personal revival to all involved. With new vision and renewed strength from God, I reached out with boldness to pastors, administrators, counselors, and friends in my community who God put in my life at that time. As it would be, they all shared the same burden and wanted to help these students be successful to reach their full potential. We believed that revival would happen as we reached out beyond ourselves to serve them. Our mission statement was simple: "Every student was one caring adult away from being a success story." Our goal was to show them that we cared, so we named our outreach program of revival, Mt. Vernon Cares. Through our love, we believed we could help these students grow strong roots of love so that they could serve their community in the upcoming years. They would flourish and thrive as love came to life!

Mt. Vernon Cares was birthed by God to help feed and mentor junior high and high school students who were at risk to graduate. I would not have had the courage or boldness to reach out to them without the *second touch* of Jesus active within me and the guidance and direction of the Holy Spirit. After I surrendered, I became new in Christ, and a new divine spark of life in Christ was born again inside me to reach those in need. I was on fire for what God wanted to accomplish. As I continued praying, Christ brought people who could help mentor and donate the funds for the monthly food vouchers. He also directed us to the many students who needed to know that someone cared. They were waiting for us and God was waiting for us to help them. It is truly amazing how the Holy Spirit will direct our actions when we let Him have control over our lives and live in the Spirit. Life in the Spirit brought new life and revival, not only to these students in need, but also to the mentors who chose to step out and mentor them.

"I will not leave you as orphans; I will come to you. Yet a little while and the world will see me no more, but you will see me. Because I live, you also will live."
John 14:18-19

At the time of writing this book, Mt. Vernon Cares has touched many lives in the six years it has been in place. Many students have graduated and are doing well in their lives because someone cared. I am so glad that I was not afraid to let the Holy Spirit show me what I needed to do for revival to begin for the youth of my community. I continually pray that God will strengthen each student and mentor so that revival continues to take place in each willing heart. God is using this program to strengthen and encourage each student for whatever challenges they may face. Together, we can help each other as one body of Christ with the *second touch* of Jesus uniting us. With one heart, we have grown closer to Christ's love and grace. As I see how God's plan has unfolded in His perfect timing, my faith has grown even stronger. As I continue to pray for these students and mentors, the Holy Spirit encourages me to keep believing in revival because I know that we are making a difference for God in His perfect timing and His divine plan. Only God can revive our hearts with His divine and powerful Holy Spirit, our Helper.

"If you love me, you will keep my commandments. And I will ask the Father, and he will give you another Helper, to be with you forever."
John 14:15-16

In addition to Mt. Vernon Cares, another spark of revival was taking place in the churches in our community because of the prayers of its people. The start of what God did began in the fall of 2015 as we planned a prayer revival gathering in our downtown square. The pastors from the local churches in our community gathered the people to pray for revival in our town in a service we called, "Prayer on the Square." This was a unique, candlelight prayer and worship service to usher in a revival planned for November. Prayer brought a new Spirit of hope within our community. More than 500 people came to pray that night in September. Something special happened in the hearts of all who attended. When two or more come together to pray for something they agree upon, the Lord is among them. The Bible tells us that, and we grasped onto that verse as we prayed together. We felt His presence as a light mist of rain fell as we prayed. Each pastor prayed for revival with a new Spirit of hope. Each person felt the presence of the Lord in an incredibly special way. I was one of the people who prayed for this revival as we came together to pray in one accord with other believers that night. We believed God had a plan for us to experience a unification in our town as we continued to seek revival.

"Again I say to you, if two of you agree on earth about anything they ask, it will be done for them by my Father in heaven. For where two or three are gathered in my name, there am I among them."
Matthew 18:19-20

After "Prayer on the Square", a group of people from different churches in our community committed to pray each week in the downtown square to see God move in our hearts and in the hearts of the people of our community. We believed God's promise to revive us again would happen as we continued our heartfelt prayers. God moved in a special way to bring our hearts together as we lifted up our prayers for revival. We are still praying each week and have been revived again and again...

God loves to hear us pray.

Jesus touches us as we pray.

The Holy Spirit revives us as we pray.

These prayers continue today, and we believe that revival has surely come to our small town through personal revival and unity among the churches to do God's work among the people. Many are finding Jesus and wanting to wake up spiritually by seeking Jesus each day. Love is present all around our small town as we seek to serve others. I know that without the *second touch* of Jesus in my heart, I would not have been able to fathom this level of revival. It is because of His presence in me, that I was able to actively see His hand upon us. Without unity of the Spirit of the Lord, this revival would not be here among us. Revival comes to those who allow a *second touch* through surrender. My prayer is that all who are reading this book will actively turn towards Jesus and let Him revive their hearts with His *second touch* of the Holy Spirit. When you do, you can be a witness to others seeking revival.

"When the humble see it they will be glad; you who seek God, let your hearts revive."
Psalm 69:32

"Eager to maintain the unity of the Spirit in the bond of peace."
Ephesians 4:3

Be a Witness With Prayer

Revival is something that keeps on happening day after day after the surrender. It is not a one-time event, but a process of sanctification each day as we grow closer to the Lord in the power of the Holy Spirit. As our faith keeps growing, our witness does as well. God wants us to let go of fear and grab hold of faith. Without faith, it is impossible to please God.

"And without faith it is impossible to please him..."
Hebrews 11:6

I aim to please God with a sincere faith and a pure heart. I know that He will keep testing my faith and challenge me to step out of my comfort zone as I seek renewal and revival. It is not always easy, but always well worth the effort. One way I have renewed my faith and deepened my relationship with Jesus has been through prayer with other people. I have seen a restoration in me as I have tuned into the Holy Spirit and let Him stretch my faith in my prayer life.

I had always been afraid to pray out loud with others because I felt like my prayers were not powerful and well stated. In fact, I deferred to other people to lead the prayers when the opportunities to pray openly in groups presented itself. I never felt confident to lead prayer before I let the Holy Spirit empower me. After my *second touch* experience, my confidence to pray in front of groups came naturally. I let the Holy Spirit lead me in the words I would say, and my fear disappeared. In the surrender of self, my prayer life deepened and my faith grew tremendously. I began to believe in the power of prayer. God wants all of His children to pray to Him. The authority of prayer is a gift that He gives us as we engage in prayer and let the Spirit lead us as we pray.

I am actively using this gift to pray with others whenever the Spirit leads me. This is my witness. I pray to reach others with the love of Jesus in a tangible way. I give them His love, and mine, as I pray with them. I pray with my family whenever I can. I pray with strangers who the Lord directs to me as I listen to His promptings. I pray for friends who reach out and ask for my prayers. I pray with people on the phone who the Lord lays on my heart to call. I pray corporately at church with prayer and Bible study groups. I pray daily with friends who minister to me with their prayers. I pray with my husband who comforts me with his loving prayers. I also have prayed on platforms given to me by the Lord through the radio and several podcasts. **I will not stop praying!** My Bible has a note written inside of it from my daughter when she was seven years old that simply says, **"Always pray!".** She knew that prayer changes things because she was the gift given to my husband and me by God who heard our prayers. My mother's last text message to me before she passed away into the arms of Jesus was just these two words, **"Keep praying".** She knew the strength God had given her the last months as she struggled with cancer was gifted to her by God as people continued praying for her.

Prayer changes things and strengthens people. The Holy Spirit encourages me to keep being a witness for Him all the days of my life. As I continue praying, I believe I will see even more miracles! I have seen God move in mighty ways because of the faithful prayers of His people. God wants you to pray as well. He needs us to be a praying people who believe that there is power in the name of Jesus. He wants our churches to be houses of prayer. Let your spirit-filled prayers be your witness and go as the Spirit of God leads you to pray!

"But you will receive power when the Holy Spirit has come upon you, and you will be my witnesses..."
Acts 1:8

"Rejoice always, pray without ceasing, give thanks in all circumstances; for this is the will of God in Christ Jesus for you."

1 Thessalonians 5:16-18

Share Your Story for God's Glory

In addition to prayer, Jesus touches us so that we can help other people find Him again and again. He wants us to tell our story of our faith journey for His glory. He needs us to be His hands and feet as we serve others. He yearns for us to love like He loves. He hopes that we spend time sharing his love. He will strengthen us when He calls us. He will direct and connect us to those we can help disciple and mentor. He will put people in our life who need Jesus. He will give us the courage to speak and the knowledge to share. As we grow closer to Him, we will find that we want to share what we have found to be true: there is power in the name of Jesus through the Holy Spirit. The *second touch* of Jesus empowers us to go even when the world tries to hold us back.

Who in your life *needs* to know the love of Jesus?

Who *wants* to know about the hope that is within you because of Jesus?

Who *needs* a renewed faith because they have drifted from Jesus?

Who can you share with about *your* walk with Jesus?

What is *your* story?

Share your story for God's glory!

"Come and hear, all you who fear God, and I will tell what he has done for my soul."
Psalm 66:16

My Personal Testimony
and the Power of Prayer

Here is my testimony and personal story about the power of prayer. I wanted to share this with you as proof that God does answer prayers in His will and in His perfect timing!

"And blessed is she who believed that there would be a fulfillment of what was spoken to her from the Lord."
Luke 1:45

I claimed this promise from the Lord as I prayed from my heart and heard His voice speaking truth to me through His Word. My deepest desire as a young girl was to be a mother. I knew I wanted to have several children to love. As a young bride in my twenties, my husband and I planned to have children as soon as we felt the timing was right. However, the Lord had different plans for us. Our plan to be parents was not fulfilled in *our* timing, but *His*. We tried for years with no success and many tears. I struggled to understand why everyone else I knew, or saw, was pregnant but I wasn't able to have a baby. Now I know that God wanted us to trust Him for greater blessings and trust in His timing.

We visited my doctor to seek help, and after multiple negative tests and numerous disappointments, we found out our ability to have children would be a struggle for us. Instead of worrying, I decided it was time I trust the Lord to help me. I prayed and believed that God would answer our greatest desire as a young couple. Not long after I made the decision to surrender my plans over to the Lord, He answered my prayer. I was able to get pregnant with our son, Grant. Our greatest desire to have a son came true as soon as we let the Lord work out all the plans for us in His timing. His timing is always perfect!

Thankful for our son and feeling truly blessed as parents of a healthy baby boy, we decided after a few years that it was time to have another child to complete our family. The first year of trying was not successful and I even suffered a miscarriage. Then in the second year, we decided that it just might take a little longer like the first pregnancy. But what I failed to do was pray. I just kept looking at my circumstances and feeling sorry for myself. I lost faith and I felt like a failure each time I found out I was not pregnant. After several months of no luck, again, we went to the doctor to see what we could do. To our surprise, after a few tests, I got pregnant in the second year of trying! This was a happy moment for us as we were sure this would be a healthy pregnancy.

We were overjoyed and excited as our children would be three years apart and that sounded just perfect for us! But a few months into this third pregnancy, I miscarried again. This was one of the hardest times of my life. Doctors continued to believe there was no way I could have a healthy pregnancy. I was distraught and cried in anguish. My heart was crushed again and again. I couldn't believe why God would allow this to happen to me. I wondered what I had done to deserve this agony and heartache. I was sure that God had planned for us to have another child. The doctors gave us no hope and even told us it would be impossible to have another baby.

In the next year, with broken plans and a broken heart, I decided that maybe God wanted me to start fervently praying for this child. He wanted me to pour out my heart for this child! And this time it would be different. I heard the voice of God telling me that I needed to pray with my husband. I had been praying alone but had not reached out to my husband who had the same desire as me. God wanted us to pray *together* for the deepest desire of both of our hearts.

All these years, I was drawing into myself without asking my husband to pray with me. I was leaving him out of the joy of asking for something that God wanted to give to the both of us. God was waiting for us to come to Him together and ask in the name of Jesus for what we both wanted. So right there, at that moment, we vowed that we would pray diligently every single day until God answered. We believed that He would!

"The LORD is near to all who call on him, to all who call on him in truth."
Psalm 145:18

We grew in our faith together as we prayed every single day for well over a year. And, lo and behold, joy flooded our hearts as God did answer our faithful prayers when I got pregnant with our second child, a daughter, Samantha, whose name means, "God heard." God *did* hear our prayers and answered them in a way that was better than we could have ever imagined!

Our family was complete, and our prayers were answered. When we fully trusted the Lord for His plan and prayed without ceasing, believing that God would answer our prayers, He gave us the desires of our hearts and our joy was full! Our prayers of praise continue today for our great God who answers prayers in His perfect will and perfect timing!

"Rejoice in hope, be patient in tribulation, be constant in prayer."
Romans 12:12

Do You Need the Second Touch of Jesus?

The *second touch* of Jesus is possible for all who want to have a closer relationship with Him. It starts with a desire to know Him more intimately. He wants to spend more time with all of His believers, including you. If you have the desire and passion to know Jesus, then you are ready. Come to a place where you can be still and listen with your heart. Let go of your burdens and cast them to Him. He is ready to take each concern from you. When you do, you can press on to your future. Let go and let the Spirit lead you. Where the Spirit of the Lord is, there is new life!

"Do not be anxious about anything, but in everything by prayer and supplication with thanksgiving let your requests be made known to God."
Philippians 4:6

Now, ask the Lord to touch your heart and repent of what you know you have done that is not in His will. Pray for Him to take away this shame and pattern of life. This is called surrender of your old, sinful self, much like a washing off of the dirt you are carrying and stepping into a clean new life. It could also be described as putting off your old, stained clothes and being clothed in new, clean garments of salvation! When you do this, new life will begin in you.

There are promises for you when you live in the Spirit.

There is restoration for you in the surrender.

There is a life of complete joy and peace as a new creation in Christ.

"To put off your old self, which belongs to your former manner of life and is corrupt through deceitful desires, and to be renewed in the spirit of your minds, and to put on the new self, created after the likeness of God in true righteousness and holiness."
Ephesians 4:22-24

Once you surrender, a refreshment of your soul will immediately occur. A feeling of joy will enter your heart and a peace will permanently rest in your soul forever. A warm rush of love like you have never felt before will cover your body and your heart will beat with new beats of love. This experience is the *second touch* of Jesus. You will feel His presence in your heart. It is unlike anything else you will ever experience on this earth. A touch from Heaven falls upon you when you say *yes*.

"But our citizenship is in heaven, and from it we await a Savior, the Lord Jesus Christ, who will transform our lowly body to be like his glorious body, by the power that enables him even to subject all things to himself."
Philippians 3:20-21

Now, are you ready?

Why would you not want all that is yours in Christ?

There is another touch of Jesus waiting for you. Jesus is ready to cleanse you and empower you with the Holy Spirit. You can receive Him right now. He has given you the choice to love Him.

Come to Him.

Pray to Him.

Let go.

Give Him all of you.

Find the Way, Jesus Christ.

Live in the power of the Holy Spirit.

Show Jesus that you love Him by surrendering and giving Him your heart once again, a second time, and experience the *second touch* of Jesus, the Holy Spirit alive and awakened in you. You can be reached, rescued, and restored. The choice is yours to make. Don't wait another day...today can be the beginning of a new life *in Christ* for you!

"Be filled with the Spirit."
Ephesians 5:18

"But God, being rich in mercy, because of the great love with which he loved us, even when we were dead in our trespasses, made us alive together with Christ— by grace you have been saved— raised us up with him and seated us with him in the heavenly places in Christ Jesus."
Ephesians 2: 4-6

Reflection

I have written this book to share my story about why we need a touch of Jesus upon our hearts. He touches us when we let Him reach, rescue, and restore us. My prayer, after you read this, is that you will hear and know what the Holy Spirit speaks to you about where you are in your journey. We are all in the process of being reached, rescued, or restored by Jesus. I hope my story encourages you to pursue the touches of Jesus and keep growing in your relationship with Him. With each touch, there is new hope and great joy for those who desire the higher gifts Jesus gives. You will grow a closer relationship as you seek more of Jesus in your life. I have shared my experiences of my spiritual growth and how I let Jesus reshape my life with His *first touch* and His *second touch*. **My hope is that you will be encouraged to pursue a deeper relationship with Jesus after reading this book.** I pray that my story will help you open your heart to more of Jesus so that your soul may be filled with joy. His love will change you as you say Yes to Christ! There is hope for a more fulfilling and abundant life right now!

"I came that they may have life and have it abundantly."
John 10:10

Take the first step and open your heart to Jesus. He is waiting for you. After you decide to follow Him, He will live inside of you and then He will touch you again! Living with the *second touch* of Jesus means that you have not only invited Jesus to live in your heart through faith, but also, you are living in the power of the Holy Spirit engaged within you. In other words, that *second touch* empowers you and reaches deep down in your soul and directs all your thoughts, feelings, emotions, and actions. After His touch, you will be made new *in Christ* as He lives in your heart with His power at work in you. You will desire Him more and your faith will grow as you trust and obey Him. You will believe He loves you unconditionally and you will be able to rest in His love. You will be connected to Jesus through the Holy Spirit empowered within you!

Prayer for Spiritual Strength

"For this reason I bow my knees before the Father, from whom every family in heaven and on earth is named, that according to the riches of his glory he may grant you to be strengthened with power through his Spirit in your inner being, so that Christ may dwell in your hearts through faith-that you, being rooted and grounded in love, may have strength to comprehend with all the saints what is the breadth and length and height and depth, and to know the love of Christ that surpasses knowledge, that you may be filled with all the fullness of God. Now to him who is able to do far more abundantly than all that we ask or think, according to the power at work within us, to him be the glory in the church and in Christ Jesus throughout all generations, forever and ever. Amen."
Ephesians 3:14-21

"I have decided to follow Jesus.

I have decided to follow Jesus.

I have decided to follow Jesus.

No turning back. No turning back."

This precious hymn was based on the last words of a man named Nokseng who lived within the Garo tribe in Assam, India around 150 years ago. Through the sharing of the gospel by a believer in Christ, Nokseng became an ardent follower of Jesus. Because of his refusal to deny Jesus as his Lord and Savior, Nokseng faced death and the death of his family. Asked a final time to renounce Jesus, he refused, and these words poured from his lips.

I have decided to follow Jesus.

Nokseng and his family died for their faith, but his love and decision to follow Jesus sparked a revival in the hearts of his tormentors and the rest of his tribe. The whole tribe would then come to know Jesus because of this one man's incredible faith and testimony!

What about you?

Will you decide to follow Jesus?

My prayer is that you will decide to follow Jesus and let His touch activate and renew your faith. Let Jesus touch you again now with his "second touch"....

In Christ,

Jill Lowry

Jill Lowry

Looking for More?

A Year of Daily Devotionals for One-on-One
Time with God

Available on Amazon

https://www.amazon.com/dp/B08LTRBDN5

Second Touch of Jesus

God-Size Your Prayers to
Find Your Destiny

Prayers
FROM THE
HEART

Available on Amazon
https://www.amazon.com/dp/B07TW7YMHV

Also By Jill Lowry

A Year of Daily Devotionals to
Ignite Your Heart for Jesus

Available on Amazon
https://www.amazon.com/dp/B07HKK2MN9

Available on Amazon
https://www.amazon.com/dp/B079VTNMY9

Prayer Journals also Available on Amazon

https://www.amazon.com/dp/1693027763

https://www.amazon.com/dp/0578633906

ABOUT THE AUTHOR

Jill Lowry is an ardent follower of Jesus who has a desire and passion to communicate His truth. Inspired by the Holy Spirit, her writings combine the accuracy of a scholar with the practicality of a wife and mother. Jill grew up in San Antonio, Texas. She graduated from the University of Texas with a Bachelor of Business Administration in Marketing and holds a law degree from St. Mary's University School of Law.

Jill is the founder and president of a student mentoring and food program, Mt Vernon Cares, created for at-risk students at the local Junior High and High School. She is one of the hosts of a faith-based weekly radio talk show and podcast, Real Life Real People Radio. https://www.realliferealpeopleradio.podbean.com

She also co-hosts another podcast, Journey with Jesus, where two friends share truths and positivity about how to find joy in Jesus. https://podcasts.apple.com/us/podcast/journey-with-jesus-praises-and-positivity

In addition, Jill is a contributing partner on Bible.com where you can read more of her devotionals.

Jill takes every opportunity to pray with friends and neighbors in need and considers intercessory prayer a vital part of her ministry. She is part of a weekly community prayer group which meets on the Downtown Square to pray for revival in her community and beyond.

Visit her website for more information on these ministries and subscribe to receive inspirational daily prayers. http://www.jilllowryministries.com

Made in the USA
Columbia, SC
30 May 2021

38316151R00069